CANDLESTICK CLARITY

THE COMPLETE BEGINNER'S PATTERN RECOGNITION BLUEPRINT FOR READING MARKET PSYCHOLOGY AND TIMING WINNI

RILEY WHITMAN

Copyright © 2025 BY SYNAST PUBLISHING

Published by SYNAST PUBLISHING

ISBN: 978-1-968418-54-0

Table of Contents

CANDLESTICK CLARITY

Introduction vi

Embracing the Basics of Candlesticks 1

    Understanding Candlestick Anatomy 1

    Bar and Line Charts vs. Candlesticks 3

    Psychology Behind Candlesticks 4

    Common Misconceptions and Pitfalls 6

Mastering High-Probability Patterns 8

    Top Bullish Patterns for Beginners 8

    Essential Bearish Patterns 10

    Pattern Prioritization for Consistent Wins 11

    Avoiding Overwhelm with Pattern Shortlists 13

Pattern Recognition in Real Markets 15

    Live Chart Pattern Scanning Techniques 15

    Navigating Messy Market Conditions 17

    Pattern Reliability in Various Market Types 18

    Dodging Bull and Bear Traps 20

Integrating Indicators for Better Signals 23

    Using Moving Averages with Candlesticks 23

    RSI and Stochastic for Pattern Confluence 25

    Volume Analysis Essentials 26

    Multi-Timeframe Confirmation Techniques 28

Setting Up Your Trading Environment 32

Platform-Specific Setup Guides 32

Customizing Indicators and Overlays 34

Troubleshooting Common Setup Issues 35

Automating Alerts and Checklists 37

Executing Trades with Precision 40

From Chart to Trade Ticket... 40

Smart Stop-Loss Placement.. 42

Confirmation Entries and Exits 43

Volume and Trendline Validation 45

Risk Management and Resilience 47

Calculating Risk/Reward Ratios 47

Position Sizing Strategies... 49

Adapting to Volatility and Liquidity 50

Learning from Losses... 52

Building a Personalized Trading Plan 54

Creating a Candlestick-Driven Strategy 54

Incorporating Daily Routines 56

Using Trading Plan Templates 57

Ongoing Review and Adjustment 59

Real-World Application Across Markets 61

Pattern Adaptation for Stocks, Forex, and Crypto 61

Timing Trades for Optimal Success... 63

Platform-Specific Execution Examples....................................... 64

Case Studies of Successful Trades 66

Advanced Techniques for Mastery 68

Multi-Candle Patterns and Their Uses 68

Pattern Journaling for Continuous Improvement 70

Leveraging Community Feedback 71

Avoiding Burnout and Maintaining Focus 73

Utilizing Technology for Enhanced Trading 75

Automated Pattern Recognition Tools 75

Backtesting Without Coding 77

Data-Driven Decision Making 78

Building a Pattern Scorecard 80

The Art of Continuous Learning 82

Keeping a Trading Journal 82

Staying Sharp with Pattern Drills 84

Adapting to Market Changes 85

Advanced Study Resources 87

Psychology and Discipline in Trading 89

Understanding Emotional Pitfalls 89

Strengthening Trading Discipline 91

Stress Management Techniques 92

Building Emotional Resilience 94

Conclusion and Next Steps 96

Recap of Key Concepts 96

Applying Knowledge in Live Markets 97

Setting Personal Trading Goals 99

Invitation to the Trading Community 101

EPILOGUE 103

INTRODUCTION

In the chaotic world of trading, understanding market movements and timing your trades can often feel like navigating a labyrinth without a map. Many beginners find themselves overwhelmed by the sheer volume of information, bombarded with complex charts, and conflicting advice, which can lead to a sense of paralysis. This book is designed to cut through the noise and provide a clear path forward.

"Candlestick Clarity" is designed to demystify the art of reading candlestick patterns, providing a comprehensive framework for traders committed to understanding market psychology and refining their timing strategies. This guide addresses the common struggles traders face, including deciphering complex jargon and identifying reliable patterns amid market fluctuations. By focusing on high-probability setups and integrating real-world examples, it transforms abstract concepts into actionable insights.

The book is structured to build your confidence and skill from the ground up. It starts with the fundamentals of candlestick anatomy, explaining how each component reflects the ongoing battle between buyers and sellers. As you progress, you'll learn to identify key patterns that signal potential market shifts, supported by data-driven analysis and practical exercises.

Furthermore, "Candlestick Clarity" emphasizes the importance of risk management, offering strategies to protect your capital while maximizing profit potential. The book includes detailed sections on integrating candlestick analysis with other indicators, providing a comprehensive approach to trading across various asset classes, including stocks, forex, and cryptocurrencies.

For those eager to apply their newfound knowledge, the book offers interactive elements, including downloadable templates and pattern recognition drills, that encourage readers to engage actively and apply the concepts in real trading environments. By the end of this journey, readers will not only have a deeper understanding of candlestick patterns but also the confidence to make informed trading decisions and navigate the markets with precision.

RILEY WHITMAN
CANDLESTICK CLARITY

1

EMBRACING THE BASICS OF CANDLESTICKS

Understanding Candlestick Anatomy

Candlestick charts are a vital tool for traders, providing a graphical representation of price changes over time. Every candlestick in these charts comprises multiple main elements, providing important information about market dynamics. Any trader who wishes to understand market psychology and make informed trading decisions needs to comprehend these components.

The main constituents of a candlestick are the body and wicks, or shadows. The body is a measure of the variance between the opening and closing prices of a trading session. A filled or solid body implies that the closing price was less than the opening price, implying bearishness. On the other hand, a hollow or unfilled body indicates that the closing price is greater than the opening price, indicating a bullish market. The body length may provide some insight into the intensity of selling or buying pressure. A long body represents high momentum in the direction of the candle, whereas a short body indicates indecision or weak momentum.

The upper and lower wicks are extensions of the body. These are the maximum and minimum prices that were achieved during the trading period. The upper wick indicates the highest price at which sellers had driven the price down, and the lower wick represents the lowest price at which buyers had forced the price up. The length of these wicks may reflect the volatility and market sentiment. With long wicks, there is high price volatility, and it may exhibit reversals. Short wicks, on the other hand, indicate steady price movements.

Every candlestick is a story of the battle between buyers and sellers. An example of this is having a long lower wick and a small body at the top of a candlestick, which could indicate that sellers initially forced the price down, but buyers regained control by the end of the day. Such candlesticks may indicate a possible bullish reversal because they reflect the strength of buyers in resisting sellers.

Grouping of candlesticks may indicate the larger market tendencies and change of heart. e.g., a sequence of candlesticks containing increasingly longer bodies, all of the same direction, may indicate a powerful trend. In contrast, alternating long and short bodies may indicate market uncertainty or a possible reversal. The patterns can only be identified through experience and keen insight because the market can often be a complex web of indicators.

Knowledge of candlestick anatomy is not limited to pattern recognition. It is about deciphering the psychology of the market forces. Every element in a candlestick captures the behavior and feelings of traders, and it is determined within a single trading period. Through the analysis of these factors, traders can gain insight into the market's mood, forecast potential price movements, and make informed trading decisions.

The candlestick analysis requires a level of technical expertise, combined with a sense of market psychology, to effectively incorporate it into the trading strategy. Understanding the importance of every element of a candlestick enables traders to predict market trends and take action before they occur. By learning to read candlesticks, traders can navigate market complexities with greater confidence and accuracy, ultimately achieving improved trading performance.

Bar and Line Charts vs. Candlesticks

In the world of financial charting, it is not a question of personal taste between bar charts, line charts, and candlestick charts. All types of charts have their unique benefits and drawbacks, which determine the way traders process and analyze market information. Bar and line charts may not be as detailed in information as candlesticks, which is vital in interpreting market dynamics and market sentiment.

Bar charts consist of vertical lines, which define the price range for a specific period, and horizontal dashes that signify the opening and closing prices. This format provides a clear picture of the price movement over time, but it tends to blur the finer aspects of market sentiment. Line charts, being simpler still, draw a single line that connects adjacent closing prices, providing a simplified visual analysis of the general price patterns. Nevertheless, this simplicity may also be a negative feature, as the line charts fail to indicate intra-period price moves, as well as opening prices, which can provide an incomplete picture of market activity.

Conversely, candlestick charts are more helpful in enabling traders to visualize market psychology due to their unique structure. The candlestick is used to represent a particular time frame, but the open, high, low, and close are all contained in one item. The candlestick body, which may be hollow or filled, represents the difference between the opening and closing prices, whereas the wicks or shadows represent the highs and lows. In this way, traders can easily determine the market's mood and identify potential turning points.

The most valued features of candlesticks include their ability to indicate patterns that may signal market reversals or continuations. Dojis, engulfing patterns, and hammers are examples of patterns that can help in timing a change in market sentiment. An example is the doji, where the difference between the opening and closing prices is small or even nonexistent, indicating market uncertainty that may lead to a reversal. In contrast, a pattern characterized by a small body and a long lower wick may indicate a bearish downward trend, as buyers are unwilling to participate in the market.

The amount of information packed into a candlestick renders it an effective tool that can be used by traders who employ technical analysis to make informed decisions. Candlestick charts enable traders to predict the market's direction more precisely than bar or line charts by providing insight into the struggle between buyers and sellers. This is especially necessary in volatile markets, where understanding the sentiment underlying a particular trade can mean the difference between making or missing a profitable opportunity.

Candlestick charts, regardless of their complexity, have become the international standard for active traders across all asset classes, including stocks, forex, and cryptocurrencies. Their ability to present all market information concisely and efficiently makes them essential in the toolkit of any trader. The more traders learn to read candlestick patterns, the more they will be able to navigate market complexities and make more strategic decisions when they understand market psychology. Therefore, bar and line charts still have their role to play in financial analysis. However, the transparency and detail provided by candlesticks still make them the option of choice when individuals want to master the art of trading.

Psychology Behind Candlesticks

The candlestick on a trading chart is not simply a graphic display of the change of prices; it is the mirror of the psychology of the members of the market. The fighting between bulls and bears as they strive to have a say in the direction of the market can be summarized in a single candlestick. It is this microcosm of trading dynamics that the true nature of candlestick patterns is based on, including the emotions, decisions, and responses of traders at any given point in time.

Take a look at the anatomy of a single candlestick: the body, wicks, and color. The body indicates the opening price and the closing price, which means the overall outcome of the trading activity in a specific period of time. A long body indicates a high buying or selling pressure, whereas a short body indicates a lack of direction or consolidation. The wicks/shadows represent the peak and trough prices of the trading session, providing information on the session's volatility and range. A long wick may indicate a reversal of price levels or rejection of price levels, indicating that the market does not want to maintain some price levels.

Groups of candlesticks represent the significant shifts in market sentiment, momentum, and the potential presence of traps. For example, the increase in confidence and optimism among buyers may be reflected in a sequence of bullish candles. In contrast, a series of bearish candles indicates an increase in fear or pessimism. Such clusters may also indicate panic selling due to fear-induced irrational behavior or spikes of unsustainable, greed-induced price rises. Understanding these collective behaviors enables traders to anticipate changes in the crowd's behavior, offering a strategic advantage in decision-making.

Patterns also reveal the psychology behind candlesticks, which indicates possible reversals or continuations. An example of a bullish engulfing pattern is when a larger bullish one follows a small bearish candle. Within this bullish candle, the earlier bearish candle is completely engulfed. This trend indicates a shift in sentiment from selling to buying, typically occurring at the end of a downward trend. A bearish engulfing pattern is equally indicative of the reverse, a shift between buying and selling pressure, which is indicative of a possible downturn.

The most common pitfalls among traders include incorrect interpretations of candlesticks, such as overreliance on patterns without considering the broader market environment. An example of a doji is regarded as a sign of indecisiveness, but its significance depends on where it is placed in the trend. A doji on its own might not portend much, but when it occurs at a major support or resistance point, it may signal a major turnaround. The cost of such errors is too high; therefore, it is essential to have a detailed explanation of not only the candlesticks themselves, but also their contextual meaning.

Lastly, understanding the candlesticks well can give one an advantage over other investors who may only use the lagging indicators. Although technical indicators have their place, in most cases, they are used to confirm what the candlestick already represents. By paying attention to price action and the psychology it conveys, traders can operate with greater confidence and accuracy, thereby avoiding the pitfalls and fake outs that plague less informed market participants. This psychological observation transforms candlestick analysis into an effective method for interpreting and forecasting market trends, rather than merely a charting method.

Common Misconceptions and Pitfalls

Candlestick patterns have been regarded with a tint of mystery and possibilities, especially in the field of trading. However, this attraction may sometimes mislead traders into giving false impressions that can prove detrimental to their trading success. These misconceptions are crucial for any trader to understand in order to navigate the markets with clarity and accuracy.

The most commonly known myth by traders is that all candlestick patterns are a sure profit indicator. The belief is usually based on the simplification of trading techniques, with the use of patterns such as the doji or the engulfing serving as individual signals of market turning points or market continuation. But the truth of the matter is that there is no foolproof candlestick pattern. The success of a pattern is highly related to the contexts within which it exists. Factors such as market trends, volume, and market sentiments are essential determinants of a pattern's viability.

The second pitfall is overfitting or attempting to impose patterns on charts. Traders may be keen to see a pattern in a market where one does not exist, as they seek to find a pattern that aligns with their expectations. This overfitting will result in poor trading decisions, as the patterns identified are not, in most cases, backed by the underlying market dynamics. The risk here is that of confirmation bias, where traders carefully attend to evidence that confirms their initial beliefs and disregard conflicting data.

The problem of hindsight bias also ruins the analysis of candlestick patterns. A historical chart is a common tool that traders use to view and observe some patterns that seem to have accurately predicted market trends. This ex post facto transparency is deceptive. Patterns in real-time trading are never as obvious, and market noise can easily distort the indicators. The bias may cause the traders to overrate the predictability of patterns and underrate the complexity of real-time market circumstances.

Furthermore, most traders often overlook the broader market context when examining candlestick patterns. A trend that appears to be a break in a transitioning market could be a momentary rest, rather than a permanent shift. The inability to factor in variables such as support and resistance rates, economic announcements, and general market sentiment may result in misinterpretation and costly errors.

Traders can avoid these traps by taking a big-picture approach to pattern analysis. It involves combining candlestick patterns with other technical indicators and market analysis tools to verify signals and enhance their reliability. An example of this approach is to employ volume analysis to estimate the strength of a pattern or to use moving averages to establish the direction of the trend, thereby eliminating false signals and enhancing informed decision-making.

Moreover, traders are expected to develop a disciplined approach to thinking, whereby they are keen on pattern confirmation and wait until further confirmation is part of the signal before taking action. This forbearance can be used to avoid premature entries and exits that occur frequently when traders act on impulse, reacting to any perceived pattern formation and proceeding before confirmation.

Ultimately, the key to avoiding such pitfalls and misconceptions is to learn and adapt to new information. Through journaling on their trades, examining their previous trades, and being open to new knowledge, traders can enhance their understanding of candlestick patterns and develop a more sophisticated trading strategy. This is a continuous process of learning and adaptation that is crucial to long-term success in the changing world of market trading.

2

MASTERING HIGH-PROBABILITY PATTERNS

Top Bullish Patterns for Beginners

The use of candlestick patterns is a crucial technical analysis tool that helps traders gain insight into the market's mood and potential direction. The bullish trends are especially important among them, as they allow recognizing when to join the market at the right time, expecting that prices are going to rise. These patterns are crucial for beginners, and understanding them forms the foundation for more advanced trading techniques.

The Bullish Engulfing pattern is a pattern that new traders will learn the most. It includes two candles, with the second candle entirely covering the body of the first, indicating a potential shift from a downward trend to an upward trend. This trend is strong, as it indicates a significant reversal of the trend, with buyers dominating sellers, suggesting a bullish future. The best arrangement occurs when the pattern is displayed following a strong downward trend, accompanied by an increase in volume to support the effectiveness of the reversal.

The other critical pattern is the Hammer, which features a short body and a long lower wick created at the bottom of a downtrend. Its long wick implies that the sellers were forcing the price downward, but buyers succeeded in restoring it to the original condition, and the price ended close to the initial price. This means that there is possible buying pressure and a potential reversal. The effectiveness of the Hammer is increased when it appears at support levels or when it has been on a downward trend but has been declining over a prolonged period, indicating that the downward trend may be losing momentum.

A three-candle structure, known as the Morning Star pattern, provides a strong signal of a potential reversal. It has a long bearish candle with a small-bodied candle in between (either bearish or bullish), and finally ends in a long bullish candle that well extends into the body of the first candle. This trend indicates that the selling pressure is diminishing and buyers are gaining control. The Morning Star is most effective when it occurs at the end of a downtrend and is supported by an increase in trading volume.

The other two-candle formation that indicates possible bullishness is the pattern known as the Piercing Line. It begins with a long bearish candle, followed by a bullish candle that opens below the low of the former candle and closes above its midpoint. This trend indicates a reversal, as selling pressure is shifting to buying interest. The Piercing Line is especially dependable when it occurs following a period of decline, as the second candle tends to end close to the day's highs.

Lastly, the Bullish Harami is a two-candle structure in which a small bullish candle wholly encloses the body of the previous larger bearish candle. This trend is an indication of market hesitation, with the sellers now turning to buyers. It is one indication that the current downward trend may be losing strength, particularly when it occurs at support areas or after a sharp downward movement.

To the novice, the challenge of learning these patterns consists not only in identifying their shapes and occurrences but also in understanding the context in which they occur. At the same time, additional confirmation can be obtained by studying volume, trend strength, and support and resistance levels to enhance the chances of making successful trades. With these major bullish patterns in mind, new traders have the opportunity to establish a strong foundation for further technical analysis and enhance their market decision-making.

Essential Bearish Patterns

Bearish patterns are crucial in the trading arena because they signal impending downtrends in the market's mood. When these patterns are identified at the right time, they can provide traders with the opportunity to capitalize on any declining price trends. These patterns can only be understood with a keen sense of observation and a thorough understanding of the market's psychology.

One of the well-known patterns among traders is the bearish Engulfing Pattern. It takes place when a little bullish candle is then succeeded by a bigger bearish candle that fully covers the body of the former candle. This tendency indicates a reversal of the mood between bullish and bearish, meaning that the sellers have outperformed the buyers. The psychological basis of this pattern suggests a reversal of trend, which is often validated by a further decline in price.

Another important trend is the Shooting Star, which typically appears in an uptrend. The pattern consists of a small body and a long upper wick, resembling a star falling from the sky. The long wick indicates that buyers increased the price well above the previous session. Still, at the end of the session, sellers decreased the prices, representing a loss of momentum and the possibility of a reversal. The Shooting Star can be a strong signal of the fatigue experienced by buyers, typically resulting in a decline in prices.

The Evening Star pattern is a three-candle formation that indicates a powerful reversal. It started with a big bullish candle, followed by a smaller one, and then finally a big bearish one. The indecisive middle candle sets the stage for the next bearish candle, which further confirms the pattern. It is an influential indicator of a trend direction change, typically marking the peak of an upward trend.

Another very important bearish pattern that traders need to be aware of is the Dark Cloud Cover. This trend is observed when a bearish candle is opened higher than the previous bullish candle but is closed lower than its midpoint. This trend indicates that the bears have staged a takeover, and the price has decreased, potentially leading to further losses. It indicates a change of direction, and it is common when a bullish trend is nearing its climax.

Finally, there is the Bearish Harami, a two-candle formation that also signifies a possible reversal. It starts with one huge bullish candle, and then there is another small bearish one inside that one. This trend suggests that the stock market's momentum is weakening, and a potential turnaround may be on the horizon. The psychological aspect of this pattern is the buyer's reluctance, which enables the sellers to regain control once again.

All these patterns provide traders with practical information on the market's behavior. Effective use of these patterns requires both familiarity with them and the ability to interpret them within their context. Volume, the strength of trends, and market conditions should be taken into consideration to enhance the credibility of these signals.

When it comes to trading, knowing how to identify bearish patterns on a chart is only the first step in mastering them; a lot more goes into it than that. Understanding these patterns can be considered one of the most effective tools for a trader, as it provides the possibility to predict market trends and make informed decisions. Just like any trading strategy, practice, and experience are crucial for capitalizing on the most successful trades using these patterns.

Pattern Prioritization for Consistent Wins

It may not be very clear for traders, who may be overwhelmed by the choices that will yield success when navigating the maze of candlestick patterns. Patterns in terms of statistical advantage and recognizability should be given top priority to achieve regular wins. The best approach is to weed out less certain patterns and concentrate on those with a proven track record of success.

The first step in automating pattern prioritization is to have a clear ranking system. This system will consider patterns based on their historical performance in terms of winning and the clarity of the pattern. Current patterns that have a high win rate and a unique visual impression should be given priority, as they have a higher chance of success. This will not only simplify the decision-making process but also minimize the cognitive load associated with live trading sessions.

To increase the efficiency of trade, traders are invited to develop a system of pattern shortlists. This will entail creating a small cheat card that indicates the three best bullish and bearish patterns, as well as important contextual indicators to help determine the best time to trade. A sheet like this can be used as a point of reference in a hurry, allowing the trader to easily evaluate possible configurations without being overwhelmed by unnecessary details.

Practically, using this prioritization strategy requires analyzing actual scenarios from the chart. Traders can observe the advantages of focus and clarity by contrasting cluttered charts with too many patterns and charts that display the top two most important patterns. It is both an easier way of trading and a more likely method of discovering high-quality setups.

Pattern prioritization also has the important aspect of customization. Traders are encouraged to customize their lists of patterns to ensure consistency with their individual trading preferences, trading time, and style. An example would be a swing trader who is more interested in patterns with a longer time frame and more substantial trend confirmation. In contrast, a scalper might be interested in short-term patterns that provide easy entry and exit points.

Additionally, it is recommended to use a checklist method to tailor pattern priorities according to traders' preferences. This checklist must consider various aspects, including volatility, market conditions, and individual risk tolerance. In this manner, traders will be able to narrow down their target, dealing only with setups that cater to their particular trading interests and strategies.

Ultimately, pattern prioritization aims to minimize noise and focus on configurations that yield the most consistent and reliable outcomes. By simplifying the decision-making process and focusing on high-probability patterns, traders will have an improved chance of winning in the market on a regular basis.

Avoiding Overwhelm with Pattern Shortlists

The world of candlestick patterns can be likened to a dense forest that one must navigate, with each step presenting a new range of challenges. This complication may cause one to feel overwhelmed, especially for those just starting their trading journey. Nevertheless, it can be clarified by using pattern shortlists strategically as a guide, steering the trader through the fog and enabling them to concentrate on high-probability setups.

In trading, simplicity can easily be converted into efficiency. To a large extent, traders can mitigate the issue of cognitive load associated with pattern identification by filtering out a list of patterns that have the best statistical probability of gain and are the simplest to identify. This would not only reduce the confusion that occurs when attempting to memorize all possible patterns but also increase the accuracy and speed of decision-making, which is extremely important in live trading.

Pattern shortlist: A pattern shortlist serves as a useful filter, enabling traders to focus on patterns where they are most likely to expect a positive result. This is achieved by focusing on patterns that have a proven track record of success, which can be established through historical analysis and real-world experience. Traders can also discard patterns that occur with low frequency or are less reliable, thereby reducing the complexity of their strategies and focusing on patterns that provide the most promising opportunities for profit through their trades.

A deliberate choice is made in developing a shortlist of patterns. Traders should consider factors such as the win rate and clarity of patterns. Such a ranking table can be of great use as it arranges patterns according to these metrics. Additionally, traders are invited to customize their shortlists according to their own trading preferences, such as trading timeframes and the types of assets they trade. This customization ensures that the shortlist will be relevant and efficient under various market conditions.

A printable cheat sheet of the best patterns can prove invaluable in helping with real-time decision-making. The guide can be referred to as a fast-reference tool when trading in real-time and when one needs to identify and confirm patterns as quickly as possible, without having to recall complex criteria from memory. By concentrating on fewer patterns, traders can identify high-probability setups more easily and mitigate the adverse impact of information overload.

The practicalities of trading situations often reveal the advantages of a simplified approach. When comparing a messy chart with numerous patterns and a clear setup featuring just two optimal patterns, it becomes evident that having a specific strategy and a set of well-defined patterns is more beneficial. Not only does the latter make the analysis easier, but it also increases the likelihood of successful trades, as setups that are most likely to result in a successful trade are given priority.

The pattern shortlist is not an inanimate tool that must always remain unchanged, but rather a living resource that evolves with the trader's experience and market shifts. It is essential to regularly review and update the shortlist to ensure it aligns with current market conditions and the evolving skills and strategies of the trader. With this strategy, traders can navigate the intricacies of candlestick patterns with greater confidence and clarity, transforming potential overwhelm into an orderly and effective trading approach.

3

PATTERN RECOGNITION IN REAL MARKETS

Live Chart Pattern Scanning Techniques

Real-time chart pattern recognition is a crucial skill for any trader in the dynamic trading world, enabling them to make well-informed decisions. Learning to perceive patterns in the noise of live markets is an undertaking that can only be accomplished with a fine eye and a disciplined manner. Trading is a reality, and the patterns are not the transparent, textbook-ideal version one can find in schoolbooks. Traders will need to understand how to identify these patterns as they form, using partial candles, overlapping signals, and market noise to do so.

The first stage in mastering live chart pattern scanning is understanding the circumstances under which a pattern is likely to occur. This involves identifying the dominant trend and the primary areas where trends are anticipated to emerge. Traders typically begin with the overall market trend and then scale down to specific regions where price activity is likely to shift or persist. This will ensure that traders are not just responding to single candles but rather taking into account the broader market situation.

After creating a context, pattern qualifiers are then searched. These constitute set standards that a pattern has to fulfill in order to be tradable. An example of this is a bullish engulfing pattern that requires a follow-up close higher than the pattern itself. In live trading, traders tend to use a systematic scan of every conceivable pattern according to their own criteria. This discipline method will help eliminate false signals and focus on high-probability setups.

Live pattern recognition is a skill that can be perfected with the use of visual drills and exercises. Such exercises simulate actual trading and test traders' ability to identify patterns within a given timeframe on various charts and timeframes. For example, a trader might be training to spot patterns on a 1-minute chart while a countdown timer is running. These exercises develop the quickness and precision of successful pattern identification in live markets.

Pattern scanning involves troubleshooting. Markets are often complex, and patterns may be unclear or emerge across multiple candles. Traders must develop a sense of when to abandon a trade due to uncertain setups. A personalized list of when to pass may be a useful aid, as this would allow the traders to avoid setups that fail to meet their expectations or are plagued by overlapping indicators.

Additionally, it is necessary to understand pattern reliability. Traders must understand the statistical probability of various patterns, such as win rates and average risk-to-reward ratios. This knowledge enables traders to perceive certain patterns as more significant than others, based on market conditions and their personal experiences.

Lastly, journaling is essential. Maintaining a comprehensive record of trends followed and the trading history they create will help the trader refine their strategy over time. By monitoring the most effective patterns under specific circumstances, traders can continuously enhance their pattern recognition abilities and make more informed trading decisions. It is through this continuous learning and adaptation that mastery in the art of live chart pattern scanning is achieved.

Navigating Messy Market Conditions

Market conditions are often likened to a stormy sea in the uncertain world of trading, and traders need to navigate through it. The higher the volatility, the more inconsistent the candlestick patterns are, and the wicks are much longer, as well as the bodies are distorted, because the market is uncertain. Such volatility may turn an otherwise simple trend into a false alarm, and the most seasoned traders can be put to the test.

In such circumstances, traders must find ways to adjust their strategies, recognizing that established rules may no longer be applicable. The wick length and candle bodies may be exaggerated, which can result in traps. An occurrence that has been known to signal continuation or reversal may now show indecisiveness, and traders should be cautious and patient.

The false out, or fake out, is one of the biggest traps in volatile markets, whereby a trend appears to be working as a pattern, then turns and leaves traders holding on the wrong side of the pattern. Long wicks and quick turns are hallmarks of these kinds of environments, and they are often exacerbated by a lack of liquidity or a news event that drives the price in an upward or downward direction with no predictable outcome.

Traders who want to navigate through such turbulent waters are encouraged to realign their pattern filters and confirmation requirements. Using longer periods can help remove noise, providing a clearer view of the underlying trend. The risk of trading based on false signals can be reduced by waiting for multi-candle confirmation, particularly in cryptocurrencies.

Under such circumstances, risk management is of utmost importance. Potential losses can be mitigated by wider stop losses or fractional position sizing. It is also recommended not to trade during scheduled news releases, as they may increase market volatility and cause unexpected price shifts.

Knowing the most appropriate times of the day and week to be reliable in patterns can also enhance a trader's strategy. The reliability of candlestick patterns is greatly influenced by market open and close times, such as the power hour in U.S. stock markets or the overlap between the London and New York sessions in the forex markets. Identifying the time when patterns are most likely to work or fail can be a significant advantage to traders.

Additionally, weekends, holidays, and overlaps between sessions have a significant impact, particularly in the cryptocurrency and foreign exchange (forex) markets. It is more likely to find fake outs when liquidity is thin on weekends in crypto markets and volatility spikes when handing off sessions in forex. A cheat sheet of the optimal timing for each market can be a handy guide to the most and least favorable times to trade.

Traders may be better positioned to benefit from opportunities and mitigate risk by understanding and adapting to these disorganized market conditions. It is essential to strike a balance between rigidity and adaptability, and it is crucial to evaluate the market landscape and adjust strategies accordingly continually. Trading success does not solely lie in the ability to recognize certain patterns, but also in understanding the context in which these patterns appear and being ready to adjust the approach when the market dictates.

Pattern Reliability in Various Market Types

The candlestick patterns used in technical analysis have varying levels of reliability depending on the market in which they are applied. The different market types (stocks, forex, and cryptocurrencies) are associated with unique attributes that affect the effectiveness of these patterns. It is essential to understand these nuances in order to develop more effective strategies and improve the success rate of traders.

Candlestick patterns, such as bullish engulfing and the morning star, have been widely regarded as reliable predictors of market sentiment in stock markets where trading occurs during specific hours and with comparatively high liquidity. The systematic structure of stock markets is more likely to favor the development of more apparent patterns, as the opening and closing prices of stocks provide more specific data, which can be used to construct candlestick bodies and wicks. Additionally, institutional investors and regulated trading hours make the stock market even more stable, allowing for more predictable patterns that are less likely to be erratic.

On the other hand, the forex market is 24-hour in nature, and the volume of trading is highest during the overlapping trading sessions of the major financial centers. This 24-hour trading environment may cause greater volatility and liquidity, which can distort candlestick patterns. For example, pin bars and dojis, which signal possible reversals, may be more prevalent due to the high volatility in prices triggered by news releases or economic data announcements. Forex traders commonly use multi-timeframe analysis to verify patterns employing longer timeframes to filter the noise of shorter-term charts. The volatility of currency pairs necessitates a flexible approach to working with candlestick analysis, where volume and trend strength play a crucial role in confirming patterns.

The cryptocurrency markets present an entirely different challenge. Being highly volatile and decentralized, such markets may generate exaggerated wicks as well as false breakouts, and the reliability of patterns is particularly a big issue in these volatile markets. The trends that traders in the crypto world typically face are low liquidity and the impact of large, single transactions, which can affect price movement. Therefore, there is a likelihood that patterns such as the Hammer or shooting star do not work as anticipated, and traders must adjust to fit the new signs by integrating other indicators, such as moving averages or RSI. The 24/7 trading cycle and exposure to rapid, news-driven fluctuations also complicate the reliability of patterns in cryptocurrencies, requiring a careful and dynamic trading strategy.

The credibility of candlestick patterns is also influenced by the overall market environment, including the prevailing bullish or bearish trend, as well as the presence of support and resistance lines. Patterns are likely to be more predictable when they occur in accordance with current trends or at important technical levels, where market psychology also plays a significant role. For example, a bullish engulfing pattern on a long-term support level in an upward market has a higher chance of success in a trade than the same pattern in a hilly, directionless market.

The time limitation of analysis is also a consideration that traders must take into account. Patterns identified over longer time periods tend to be more reliable because more data points are accumulated, which helps eliminate short-term market noise. This, however, comes at the expense of diminished trading opportunities. A shorter period, on the other hand, can provide more frequent signals; however, it requires a sharp eye and a sound plan to handle the higher risk of false signals.

To sum up, candlestick patterns can be useful in understanding the market's dynamics, but their effectiveness is directly linked to the market's nature, current state, and the trader's ability to adjust their strategies in response to these factors. Traders can capitalize on candlestick patterns in various market conditions by understanding and recognizing their value.

Dodging Bull and Bear Traps

Bull and bear traps are situations in which traders find themselves in risky circumstances due to the temptation of the swiftness of returns in the trading world. These are misleading market trends that may lead unsuspecting traders to make untimely decisions. The only way to navigate such perilous waters is to develop the acuity of market psychology and technical patterns.

Bull traps are identified when a fake breakout occurs in a rising market. Consider a situation in which the price is consistently increasing, and then it begins to surpass an important resistance point. This breakout may initially appear to be a robustly bullish trend, prompting traders to enter long positions. However, when this breakout is not backed by high volume or an underlying basis, it will most likely turn back and catch the bulls who had made their purchases at the highest point. The indicators of a bull trap are opportunities where there is low trading volume on the breakout or a bearish candlestick formation followed by another bearish candlestick formation.

On the other hand, bear traps occur during downward trends, in which the price appears to fall below a critical support level, indicating additional drops. Insiders can clamor to trade short positions, anticipating further decline. However, when the breakdown is not accompanied by additional selling pressure or is countered by the reversing patterns of the bulls, the price can rebound and trap the bears. The bear traps are among the traps that need to be identified by watching for signs of decreasing momentum or bullish candlestick patterns after the initial breakdown.

To successfully avoid these traps, traders should focus more on confirmation than anticipation. This implies that one must wait for another confirmation signal before making trades. An example of this is when a trader waiting for a confirmation candle would have to close below the breakout level before committing to a short. In a similar vein, to avoid bear traps, it may be prudent to wait for a confirmation candle that has closed higher than the breakdown level, then proceed to take a long position.

Volume analysis is important as it legitimizes the power of breakouts and breakdowns. A volume spike can also indicate a genuine breakout (or breakdown) that signifies strong market participation. Conversely, the absence of volume is a warning sign, suggesting that the trend may not be sustainable in the long term and could potentially turn into a downturn.

Additionally, outside influences such as economic news releases or other significant geopolitical events should not be ignored by traders, as they contribute to volatility and can produce false signals. During these periods, it is recommended not to involve trades except there is a strong cause to do so, as evidenced by strong technical evidence.

A bull and bear trap prevention strategy can only be developed through a disciplined approach to trading. This involves keeping a trading journal to record trades and review errors, making consistent improvements. With this insight into the psychological game at hand and a solid trading strategy, traders will be better equipped to avoid these traps and make more valuable decisions in the marketplace.

Ultimately, the key to avoiding bull and bear traps is patience, discipline, and a thorough understanding of market behavior. With technical analysis and a good sense of the market mood, one can more easily navigate the hurdles presented by these misleading market trends.

4

INTEGRATING INDICATORS FOR BETTER SIGNALS

Using Moving Averages with Candlesticks

Moving averages are a fundamental tool of financial analysis that provides traders with a smoother view of the price trend over time. They provide an effective system for making informed trading decisions when used in conjunction with candlestick patterns. Combining moving averages with candlesticks makes market signals clearer, allowing traders to analyze trends and possible reversals using more precise data.

The essence of moving averages lies in their ability to filter out random price fluctuations and reveal a clearer picture of the underlying trend. Moving averages form a line by averaging the price over a set number of periods, which broadly mimics the market's direction. This line forms a level of dynamic support or resistance, and traders can expect the possible price fluctuations around this line. The two major types of moving averages used in trading are the Simple Moving Average (SMA) and the Exponential Moving Average (EMA). Where the SMA averages prices across a given period of time, the EMA attaches greater importance to recent prices; therefore, it is more sensitive to new information.

When incorporating moving averages into candlestick analysis, it is essential to understand the candlesticks' position in relation to the moving average line. The hedging of candlesticks, especially when positioned above a moving average, is a sign of a positive trend, indicating that the market may be trending upward. On the other hand, candlesticks that develop below the moving average line are bearish in nature, and this implies that there would be a downward movement. Traders commonly use the 50-day and 200-day moving averages to determine the market's long-term performance. One of the popular techniques is attempting to identify crossovers, where the short-term moving average crosses above or below the long-term moving average, indicating an opportunity to buy or sell, respectively.

The combination of moving averages and candlesticks is particularly effective when verifying trading signals. An example of this is that a bullish candlestick pattern generated over an increasing moving average may offer a better setup for a long trade. Similarly, a bearish trend that establishes itself below a declining moving average can affirm the possibility of a down trade. This mixture helps traders eliminate spurious signals and focus on high-probability trades that align with the overall market trend.

Additionally, the moving averages may help traders establish entry and exit rules for trades. For example, a trader could choose to open only long positions when the price is above the 50 EMA, using it as a confirmation instrument to verify the existence of bullish trends. This strategy ensures trades are made according to the prevailing trend, thereby increasing the chances of success.

Practically, traders have the opportunity to improve their strategy by incorporating moving averages into a broader trading plan. This may involve establishing specific entry and exit rules, based on moving average crossovers and candlestick verifications. Additionally, traders can utilize moving averages to establish stop-loss and take-profit levels, ensuring their risk management approach aligns with the overall trend direction.

Ultimately, a combination of candlestick patterns and moving averages provides traders with a comprehensive analysis. It provides an equilibrium between the historical perspective on price movements and real-time data on candlestick formations. By learning to use motion averages and candlestick patterns, traders can gain a deeper understanding of market dynamics, making their trading decisions more informed and confident.

RSI and Stochastic for Pattern Confluence

The combination of the Relative Strength Index (RSI) and the Stochastic Oscillator embedded into the candlestick pattern analysis offers traders some potent instruments to recognize confluence arrangements, in which an assortment of indicators are distributed to support the probability of a successful trade. Both the Stochastic and the RSI are momentum oscillators, but they are used in different capacities to analyze market conditions.

The RSI measures the rate of change and speed of price changes, and it is primarily used to identify overbought or oversold markets. An RSI value below 30 indicates an oversold market condition, suggesting a potential buying opportunity as the market may be poised to reverse. On the other hand, an overbought state is indicated by an RSI of more than 70, suggesting a potential selling opportunity.

The Stochastic Oscillator, however, measures momentum by comparing a single closing price of a security with a series of its prices over a specified time. It is composed of two lines, representing the percentage K and percentage D, which move between 0% and 100%. Readings above 80 indicate an overbought condition, and those below 20 indicate an oversold condition. The Stochastic Oscillator also examines the rate of price changes and their direction, as compared to the RSI, which focuses on the level of the price. This makes it especially useful in determining possible reversals.

A combination of these two indicators and candlestick patterns can be very reliable in providing trading indicators. An example of this is when a bullish hammer appears on the RSI below 30; this may indicate a high-conviction long trade, as a reversal is possible given the candlestick pattern and the RSI. Likewise, a bearish engulfing pattern validated by a Stochastic crossover into overbought territory can provide an effective short signal, as the momentum change aligns with the reversal pattern.

Traders should seek a converging point between the candlestick and either the RSI or Stochastic signals to maximize the effectiveness of these indicators. This involves waiting until a pattern appears, then examining whether the RSI or Stochastic readings support the pattern. In this way, traders will be able to eliminate weak signals and focus on setups that have a better chance of success.

Oscillator confirmation is a crucial aspect of trading that is emphasized in the annotated trade examples. To take the example of a bearish doji pattern that develops without an overbought RSI value may not work since the absence of confirmation undermines the strength of the signal. A similar case is that a bullish pattern with the RSI showing no sign of oversold conditions could fail to mark the expected reversal, and thus the trade is not successful.

To simplify the process of identifying these Confluence setups, traders can create a checklist to streamline the process. This checklist must include the steps to identify the candlestick pattern, verify the readings of RSI or Stochastic, and assess the price action, trading only when all these conditions are met. Through such a systematic approach, traders will have a lower chance of entering low-probability trades and will have a better overall win rate.

RSI and the Stochastic Oscillator, when combined with candlestick patterns, provide traders with a solid framework for finding high-probability trading setups. Paying attention to the point of signal intersection allows traders to refine their decision-making process and enhance trading results.

Volume Analysis Essentials

Volume analysis is a crucial element in assessing the power and legitimacy of price patterns in the trading environment. Volume is often considered a proxy of institutional activity and belief in the strength of market involvement, and can go a long way to support the precision of candlestick patterns. Through volume, traders can determine whether the price movement is backed by genuine interest or merely a temporary fluctuation.

A key feature of volume analysis is identifying spikes or divergences that may either confirm or refute a candlestick pattern. To give an example, a bullish engulfing pattern, as well as an upward-trending volume, would typically be considered a more dependable signal of a possible increase in value. On the contrary, when such a trend is accompanied by less or no volume, it may not have the required support to continue the movement, thus increasing the possibility of a false signal.

The presence of volume divergence, where price is moving in one direction and volume is moving in the opposite direction, can be a red flag and indicate reversals or weaknesses in the dominant trend. Using the case of a bearish reversal and divergence in volume, the downward trend may not be supported and may undergo a reversal or consolidation.

Real-life examples illustrate the importance of volume in confirming patterns. The traders usually describe situations where confirmation of volume saved them from losses or gave them the courage to take advantage of winning deals. An example of this is when a pattern is ineffective at low volume but becomes effective when the volume increases. These experiences have made it clear why volume analysis should be incorporated into one trading strategy.

To successfully integrate volume and candlestick clues, traders may find a quick-reference guide helpful. This guide aims to describe the circumstances in which the volume can either prove or disprove a pattern, as well as the red flags to be taken into consideration. Such a systematic method can help traders identify low-probability arrangements and focus on opportunities with higher potential.

To conclude, volume analysis is not just another tool, but an important one in the trader's arsenal. With knowledge of and practice in volume dynamics, traders will be able to improve their decision-making process, trade more accurately, and ultimately achieve more reliable outcomes in their trading activities. When traders learn to read volume as well as candlestick patterns, they gain a greater insight into the market and are able to navigate it with more confidence and precision.

Multi-Timeframe Confirmation Techniques

Multi-timeframe analysis in the context of candlestick charting becomes one of the most important tools that allow a trader to maximize the predictability of his/her patterns. Such a technique involves analyzing candlestick charts over various time periods to establish the legitimacy of trading indicators. Traders can also achieve greater accuracy in their trading decisions by matching patterns with larger market trends, which helps them weed out false signals that can be seen in shorter time frames.

The crux of the multi-timeframe analysis is that it yields a top-down approach to market movements. With a broader time frame, traders can determine the prevailing direction, which can be viewed as a contextual background to patterns on smaller time frames. This approach ensures that trades are made in line with the current market direction, thereby increasing the likelihood of success.

Take, for example, a trader who notices a bullish hammer on a 15-minute chart. Although this trend may indicate a possible reversal, its significance becomes much more pronounced when accompanied by an uptrend, as seen on the 1-hour chart. The increased period is both a confirmation and thus increases the chances of the Hammer causing a lasting uphill trend. On the other hand, when examining a 5-minute graph, one may observe a bearish engulfing pattern and a 1-hour decline, which is a strong argument for selling, as it suggests that the timeframes are congruent and indicate the persistence of a negative force.

Multi-timeframe confirmation is a process entailing a systematic pattern validation. The traders begin by identifying a potential setup on their primary trading time frame. After this, they examine periods of time that are far in the future to ensure that the large market environment supports the expected action. This screen acts as a filter, removing patterns that do not align with the overall trend and reducing the likelihood of taking trades on temporary price movements.

To apply this method in practice, traders usually use a set of rules or a flowchart which was very simple. The first one is to identify a tendency within the trading period of interest. The trader then examines the correspondence of this pattern to the trend in a larger time frame. It is only upon the occurrence of an agreement between the two parties that the trader proceeds with the actual execution of the trade. This tempered practice not only enhances entries into trade but also fosters patience and discipline, which are essential virtues for successful trading.

Annotated chart sequences also demonstrate the use of multi-timeframe analysis. For example, a 24-hour trend chart with an uptrend will enhance confidence in the 4-hour bullish trend, whereas a pattern inconsistent with the larger time frame trend can be used as a warning. This type of visual assistance is invaluable in reaffirming the idea that time frame matching is critical to the process of determining true and false patterns.

To conclude, multi-timeframe confirmation methods can be regarded as an effective approach in a trader's arsenal, as they provide a systematic way to confirm candlestick patterns. When traders ensure that trades are executed based on the prevailing trend, they can reduce the occurrence of false signals and enhance their overall trading performance. This not only enhances the quality of trade decisions but also makes them more confident in handling the complexities of financial markets. Multi-timeframe analysis is a highly important tool in candlestick charting, as it enables traders to make their patterns more reliable and accurate. This methodology involves studying candlestick patterns at various time intervals to establish whether the trading signals are genuine. Traders can also eliminate false signals by comparing patterns to the overall market pattern, thus improving the accuracy of their trading decisions.

Multi-timeframe analysis is a unique kind, where the movement of the market is measured in a top-down fashion. Rather than making predictions in lower timeframes, traders can resort to higher timeframes to establish the trend that can serve as a background for interpreting the patterns of lower timeframes. This will ensure that trades are made in a manner aligned with the existing market trend, thereby increasing the likelihood of success.

Consider a situation where a trader has identified a bullish hammer on a 15-minute chart. Although this movement can be a sign of a potential turnaround, it is stronger by far when complemented by a rising movement on the 1-hour chart. The additional amount of time is a guarantee, which contributes to the likelihood of the Hammer causing a further upward trend. Conversely, hitting it on a 5-minute chart and in the middle of a 1-hour drop, a bearish engulfing pattern would be a good short opportunity, as the correlation between the two-time spans would indicate that the unfavorable pressure would likely continue to exist.

Multi-timeframe confirmation is a process that involves validating a pattern across multiple timeframes. Traders would begin by locating an ideal setup in their biggest trading encounter. They subsequently consider the longer durations of time so as to ascertain that the greater market setting is agreeable to the forecasted relocation. This validation procedure serves as a sieving mechanism, as it eliminates patterns that do not conform to the overall trend and reduces the risk of making trades based on short-lived price fluctuations.

To implement this approach, traders can utilize a straightforward set of rules or a flowchart to guide their decisions. The former requires pinpointing of a trend within the desired trading period. The trader will then examine how this pattern aligns with the trend over a longer period. Only where the two timeframes coincide will the trader proceed to affect the trade. Such a rigorous approach will not only enhance the quality of the trade entries but also foster traits like training and forbearance, which are valuable trade virtues.

Annotated chart sequences can also be used to describe the practical implementation of multi-time frame analysis. To illustrate this, a daily chart currently in an uptrend may reinforce the presence of a 4-hour bullish trend; however, a trend contrary to the higher time frame trend may serve as a warning. These are highly effective visual tools that enable the concept of matching that time slot to determine true and false trends.

In conclusion, multi-timeframe confirmation techniques are an efficient tool in the trader's arsenal, offering a methodological way to confirm candlestick patterns. By ensuring the trades are set according to the trend direction, where the direction is dominant, traders can minimize the number of false signals and improve their overall trading performance. Not only does it improve the quality of trade decisions, but it also provides a greater degree of confidence in understanding the complexities of the financial markets.

5

SETTING UP YOUR TRADING ENVIRONMENT

Platform-Specific Setup Guides

To gain insight and accuracy in their analysis, traders must navigate the complexity of setting up candlestick charts on various trading platforms. The features and interfaces in each platform differ, and it is essential to approach each platform uniquely to maximize the effectiveness of candlestick patterns.

On Trading View, you first enter into the charting interface, where a user is presented with a host of possibilities to customize their chart views. It is easy to choose the candlestick mode, but to make the visuals really clear, customization begins. Users can customize their color preferences, making it easy to identify bullish and bearish candles. Moreover, TradingView provides various drawing tools, which are essential for marking support and resistance levels, as well as for pattern recognition. Novices often encounter issues when resetting timelines and losing candles, which can be easily resolved by adjusting straightforward navigation settings and setting the correct timeframes.

Another widely used platform, Meta Trader, follows a somewhat different setup procedure. In this case, to switch to candlestick charts, you must use the menu settings to modify the default settings. The MetaTrader is also known for its strong capabilities in integrating indicators, allowing traders to overlay various indicators on their candlestick charts easily. The configuration of these overlays includes the way the parameters are set to avoid clutter and make the most relevant data visible. The fact that the platform supports complex configurations of indicators makes it highly popular among traders who use technical analysis to inform their investment choices. New users, however, may encounter a problem aligning these overlays, which can result from indicator lag or improper settings. These issues can be corrected by resetting chart settings to the default and properly managing templates.

Thinkorswim, which is packed with analytical tools, provides a comprehensive platform for both novice and experienced traders. To set up candlestick charts, select the chart style you prefer and adjust the candle appearance, including the color and wick thickness. The Thinkorswim interface allows for a high level of customization, enabling traders to tailor their charts to suit their strategic needs. The crucial visual aids, such as grid lines and zoom level, can be adjusted to enhance readability and ensure that significant patterns are not overlooked. The platform's advanced features, including bracket orders and trade journaling, also enable traders to execute and review their trades with greater detail and accuracy. The large number of tutorials and community forums available on the platform can be a valuable resource for beginners, addressing common problems in setting up or trading.

The need to focus on clarity and readability cannot be overemphasized on all platforms. Traders should ensure that their charts are both visually appealing and practical, effectively showcasing key market signals. Simple troubleshooting, such as verifying the presence of missing candles or illegible colors, is part of the process involved in learning platform-specific configurations. Traders can significantly enhance their analytical abilities by dedicating time to learning the specific functionalities of each platform, leading to more informed and effective trading decisions.

Customizing Indicators and Overlays

In trading, customizing charts according to individual needs is a critical skill that can significantly enhance decision-making and performance. Indicators and overlays can be completely customized, enabling traders to not only present data in a manner that fits their strategies but also eliminate market noise and concentrate on the most important signals. This individualization begins with recognizing the key features of the trading platforms and their ability to be customized to personal preferences.

The customization process begins by selecting a set of indicators that can be used to enhance the trading style. An example is a trader who emphasizes momentum, who may utilize oscillators such as the Relative Strength Index (RSI) or the Stochastic Oscillator, which provide the trader with information on whether a market is overbought or oversold. In the meantime, trend-following traders may be inclined to work with moving averages, such as the Simple Moving Average (SMA) or Exponential Moving Average (EMA), to smooth price data and define the trend direction in various time frames.

After selecting the indicators, the next step is to set the indicator settings. This includes adjusting settings such as the period length of moving averages or threshold values of oscillators, which can be tailored to market conditions or the time of day during which trading occurs. The individualization of these parameters will help match the indicators to the specific behaviors of the traded assets, thereby improving predictive accuracy.

Besides establishing indicators, traders are also supposed to pay attention to the visual appearance of the chart. This involves selecting color schemes, line thickness, and layouts. This aesthetics, although appearing superficial, are instrumental in ensuring that the chart can be read and that essential information can be identified at a glance. An example is color-coding the various moving averages according to their length, so that crossovers, commonly regarded as either buy or sell signals, can be easily spotted.

Another effective customization tool is to overlay multiple indicators into a single chart. This method enables traders to observe the intersection of signals, thereby enhancing their confidence in trade decisions. However, care should be taken not to overload the chart with too many details, which can make it difficult to analyze. The balance of a well-organized chart is to show only the required indicators that provide the trader with a complete picture of the market, without overwhelming them with excessive information.

To make charts even more useful, traders can configure alerts to notify them of important events, such as when an indicator reaches a specific level or when a crossover occurs between two indicators. This is an added advantage, especially for individuals who are unable to constantly monitor the markets. Notifications can be set to alert traders through email or the mobile application in the trading platform, ensuring they don't miss a crucial market movement.

Last but not least, traders should take advantage of the option to save their custom settings in the form of templates. This can be applied instantly to various assets or time periods, saving time and providing consistency in analysis. A wide range of trading platforms enables the creation of various templates, which can be tailored to suit different strategies or market environments, providing flexibility and responsiveness in a dynamic trading environment.

Through the art of customizing indicators and overlays, traders can transform their charts into powerful analysis tools that enable them to understand market trends better and make informed trading decisions. This personalization is not only helpful in more profound visualization, but also in more disciplined and systematic trading activities.

Troubleshooting Common Setup Issues

Managing the complexity of candlestick chart formations can sometimes pose challenges for traders, especially those unfamiliar with technical analysis. One is likely to encounter a couple of stumbling blocks along the way, and knowing how to address them can vastly improve the efficiency and experience of trading.

The loss of candlesticks or their improper placement in the chart is one of the most common problems that traders encounter. This typically occurs due to incorrect time frame settings. It is essential to ensure that the chart is adjusted to the correct time period, as various trading strategies may require different time frames to identify the optimal pattern. This problem can be easily solved by making a minor adjustment to the chart settings, which will properly align the candlesticks and provide a clearer view of the market trends.

The next most common problem is the poor presentation of colors, which may lead to misinterpretation of market indicators. Candlestick charts rely heavily on color coding to differentiate between bullish and bearish trends. This may result in misunderstandings and misguided trading moves if the color settings are not adequately set. It is essential to note that traders should customize the color scheme of their charting platform to their own preferences, making the charts easier to read and less likely to be misinterpreted.

Additionally, traders often face issues with chart clutter. This occurs due to the overlapping of too many indicators or drawings on the same chart, which makes it hard to identify the most important candlestick patterns. By simplifying the chart, its readability can be enhanced by eliminating non-relevant indicators and focusing on the most relevant ones. This is a minimalist tool that helps maintain focus on the most important patterns, which can be crucial in making informed trading decisions.

Zoom settings may also be a problem. An incorrect zoom level may either hide important information or display too much, leading to analysis paralysis. It is essential to adjust the zoom to a level where the patterns are not overly enlarged. This enables traders to see candlestick patterns clearly, making it easier to identify and analyze them.

There is also the possibility that traders may experience difficulties navigating historical data. Back-testing strategies and knowledge of historical market behavior require efficient scrolling through historical data. The effectiveness of this process can be improved by becoming familiar with the platform's navigational tools and shortcuts, allowing traders to find and analyze previous market information without unnecessary delays.

Finally, technical problems, such as platform lag or synchronization errors, can also hinder trading. These problems can be addressed by ensuring that the trading software is up-to-date and compliant with the existing system requirements. Many common technical glitches can be avoided by checking the trading system after a regular update and doing basic maintenance on it.

With these typical setup problems resolved, traders can customize their chart setups to gain a better understanding and may consequently enjoy greater success in trading. The identification and troubleshooting of these issues is a basic occurrence in learning the art of candlestick chart analysis, and is the gateway to confident and competent trading. With a simple, clean, and efficient chart structure, traders can dedicate their time to what is truly important: finding and executing profitable trades.

Automating Alerts and Checklists

Efficiency and precision are the keys in the sphere of trading. Both can be increased significantly when automated alerts and checklists help a trader incorporate them into their daily routine. Through the establishment of automated alerts, traders can be assured that they are alerted first in case of any trading opportunities and can therefore take decisive action. When properly set, these alerts serve as a watchtower, scanning the markets to identify specific conditions or patterns that support a trader's strategy.

This begins by identifying the most crucial indicators and patterns that are essential to your trading strategy. It can be the intersection of the moving averages, the breakout of a specific resistance level, or the development of a specific candlestick pattern; these criteria must be well-articulated. After this, these parameters are fed into the alert mechanism of the trading platform. Software such as TradingView, MetaTrader, and Thinkorswim offer powerful features that enable traders to configure alerts tailored to their individual needs.

These alerts are effective because they can track multiple markets and times simultaneously, which would otherwise be virtually impossible to achieve manually without risking missing some. Notifications can be activated as alerts to receive notifications by email, SMS, or directly through the trading platform, ensuring real-time information, regardless of the trader's location.

Simultaneously, checklists are a systematic method of ensuring that all aspects related to a trade are considered before it is implemented. The drawn-up checklist is a pre-flight checklist used to guide the trader through a series of steps to ensure everything is occurring as planned. This encompasses verifying concurrence across various timeframes, determining varying volume trends, and establishing risk management parameters, including stop-loss and take-profit levels.

To design a proper checklist, one must have a profound understanding of their trading strategy and the discipline to adhere to it religiously. All items on the checklist must be practical and detailed, covering various aspects of trade validation and execution. For example, a checklist may begin by ascertaining the trend over a longer timeframe, followed by confirmation of the presence of any contradictory indicators.

The checklist criteria can also be automated during their execution. On certain platforms, traders can programmatically enforce rules regarding checklists, ensuring that trades cannot be executed unless all the rules are satisfied. This will minimize the chances of making emotional or impulsive trading decisions, which are likely to result in less optimal outcomes.

In addition, these checklists may be supported by automated systems, which will enable an understanding of their efficiency and how to make them more effective. Through historical analysis of data, traders can refine their checklists to achieve better predictive accuracy and operational efficiency.

Automated alerts and checklists enable trading to become a proactive practice, rather than a reactive one, where decisions are made according to preset criteria rather than on impulse. Not only does this enhance the quality of trades, but it also gives the trader a higher sense of confidence and control, which ultimately results in more consistent and profitable trading results.

6

EXECUTING TRADES WITH PRECISION

From Chart to Trade Ticket

The ability to shift between analyzing a chart and a trade ticket is a necessary skill that requires accuracy and confidence. The analysis will begin with an in-depth examination of the chart, during which patterns are not only identified but also verified through a series of checks that demonstrate their reliability. It constitutes an in-depth evaluation of candlestick patterns, which align with macro market trends and appear to be supported by other indicators, such as volume or moving averages.

The candlestick chart, in itself, is a narrator that tells the story of the continuous struggle between buyers and sellers. Every candle captures a moment in this action, and its body and wicks reveal the intensity of the battle. The trader is required to learn to read such stories and know whether a trend indicates a continuation or a reversal of the existing trend. This knowledge plays a crucial role in determining whether to engage in trade or not.

After identifying a pattern, confirmation of its validity is the next step. It is here that the trader must utilize additional analytical tools. Spikes in volume, for example, can serve as confirmation of a pattern's strength, indicating whether institutional investors are supporting the move. On the same note, trendlines drawn on the chart may also serve as auxiliary confirmation tools, confirming or refuting trade setups.

Once the trader has verified the pattern, they then need to arrange the trade. This involves determining the exact entry and exit points based on the nature of the pattern and the trader's risk management approach. Information such as the trade price at entry, the stop-loss price, and the target to take profits is all entered in the trade ticket. These parameters are not predetermined; they are based on a thorough examination of the chart and the pattern's historical performance.

The trading process will require a platform that meets the trader's requirements, whether it is MetaTrader, TradingView, or Thinkorswim. The various platforms offer a range of tools to execute trades, starting with basic market orders and progressing to more advanced systems, such as bracket orders, which automatically establish stop-loss and take-profit levels. These platforms have a degree of complexity, and to make effective trades, it is necessary to understand them.

In addition to this, the relocation of the chart to the trade ticket is not only trivial but also psychological. The trader should have the courage to follow their analysis, believing in the patterns and their preparation. This confidence is developed over time and through practice, as well as the keeping of a detailed trading diary that documents all trades, the reasons behind each trade, and the results of those trades. These records are very useful in continuous learning and improvement of the trading strategy.

Simply put, the transition between chart analysis and trade execution is a disciplined procedure that incorporates technical analysis with a solid understanding of market dynamics and an established trading plan. It is a holistic strategy that integrates the art of pattern recognition with the science of strategic implementation, enabling traders to move the markets clearly and accurately.

Smart Stop-Loss Placement

The art of strategically placing stop-loss orders in the trading field is a process that involves striking a balance between risk management and profit opportunities. A stop-loss order is not just a catch-all; it is a deliberately considered judgment that presupposes a profound understanding of market mechanisms and candlestick patterns. This is a strategic move that is critical in saving capital and increasing the probability of winning trades.

Initiating a stop-loss order is similar to establishing a line that defines the difference between reasonable risk and perceived loss. The trick here is to place this boundary slightly higher than the important candlestick points, such as wicks, bodies, or pattern invalidation points. For example, on bullish trades, the stop-loss could be set just below the wick of a hammer candle, and vice versa. On bearish trades, the stop-loss could be placed above the high of a shooting star. This positioning will see the stop-loss follow the natural market ebb and flow, and the trader will not be subject to unjustified market noise triggers before the position is fully exhausted.

Additionally, market volatility and the timeframe of a given trade should determine the size of the stop-loss, rather than using arbitrary figures. In this respect, the Average True Range (ATR) proves useful as a measure of market volatility, enabling the determination of the stop-loss size. Through the ATR, traders will be able to place stop losses that are neither too narrow, which would result in frequent stop-outs due to market fluctuations, nor too wide, which would result in larger-than-needed losses.

The psychological factor in placing the stop-loss is also important. Traders are forced to walk the fine line between tight and loose stops. A too-tight stop can cause frequent, frustrating moves to stop and exit because of small price fluctuations, while a too-loose stop could result in excessive losses. To achieve this balance, one needs to be disciplined, and traders must measure the strength of their pattern setups and adjust their stops as the price moves in their favor.

Platform-specific guides and visual tools can enhance the accuracy of stop-loss placement. For example, trading programs such as MetaTrader and TradingView include features that enable traders to drag and move stop losses directly on the chart. The feature not only helps with accurate placement but also serves as a real-time reminder of the risk parameters associated with a trade.

Additionally, traders should avoid common pitfalls, such as placing stops on round numbers or conspicuous levels that stop hunters frequently target. These are calculated market actions designed to trigger a stop-loss order, then reverse the trend. Traders are advised to set their stops at less conspicuous levels to avoid such traps, based on the underlying candlestick patterns and the market environment.

Ultimately, the art of smart stop-loss placement is a combination of technical analysis, long-range thinking, and psychological strength. It requires traders to continually refine their strategy, based on their previous trades, and adapt to the market's dynamic conditions. Learning to place stop-losses will help traders preserve their capital and maximize the likelihood of making profitable trades, ensuring they are nimble and reactive to the constantly shifting environment of the financial markets.

Confirmation Entries and Exits

The art of confirming entry and exit points in trading is a delicate dance that cannot be mastered without understanding both the technical indicators and the psychological foundation of market movements. The main ingredient of this process is the idea of waiting until the process is confirmed, and this is an important aspect that distinguishes disciplined from impulsive traders. The concept of confirmation in trading refers to the additional information that traders seek before entering or exiting a trade, ensuring that the original pattern or signal is verified.

Traders often encounter numerous candlestick patterns that may indicate potential market movements. No confirmation, however, can prevent the tendency of such patterns from giving false signals and unprofitable trades. The confirmation process typically involves waiting until the subsequent candle closes in the direction of the expected movement. The practice can be applied to exclude noise and decrease the likelihood of generating premature signals.

An example is when a bullish engulfing pattern occurs, indicating a possible upward reversal may be underway. Nonetheless, it can be dangerous to jump into a trade as soon as a pattern is identified. Rather, it is more likely that once the next candle closes above the high of the engulfing pattern, it gives a more significant indication that the trend is actually turning. This would minimize the chances of getting caught in a bull trap in the market, where the market moves briefly and then quickly reverses.

Volume is also important in verifying entries and exits. A pattern with an impressive rise in volume denotes intense interest on the part of the market and is given more weight to the signal. An example of this is the confirmation of a bullish pattern with an ensuing candle that exhibits strong volume, indicating that the buying power behind the move is strong and that the potential trade is highly successful.

Trend lines and support/resistance levels also enhance the effectiveness of the confirmation process. A trend that is consistent with these technical indicators provides further confirmation. An example is when a breakout occurs above a resistance zone, followed by confirmation when a candle closes above the same resistance zone. This indicates an increased chance of a sustained upward trend. On the other hand, when a bearish trend is evident but the confirmation candle fails to close below a support level, it may be prudent to reevaluate the trade.

Exits, as well as entries, enjoy confirmation strategies. Technical level exit points, including past highs and lows, as well as trailing stops, can serve to capture profits and potentially realize additional gains. For instance, when a trade is in favor and approaching a major resistance level, the price activity around the level offers insight into whether to hold the trade or wait for a breakout.

Waiting to be confirmed is a very difficult discipline, particularly in fast-moving markets where a second lost is a second lost. However, this discipline is precisely what will help traders navigate the market's vagaries and irrational choices. Confirmation is merely a technical device, but it also serves as a psychological tool that keeps traders focused on their strategy rather than being swayed by market noise.

To conclude, confirmation of entries and exits is a crucial aspect of being a successful trader. It is a prudent combination of technical analysis and psychological understanding in such a way that all trades are supported with strong evidence, but not with speculation. Confirmation principles help traders enhance their decision-making process, minimize risk, and boost trading success.

Volume and Trendline Validation

As part of the technical analysis, the interaction between volume and trendlines can be used as a foundation for authenticating the candlestick patterns, which provides a stronger trading plan. Volume, which is sometimes considered the engine that drives price action, serves as a gauge of market interest and sentiment. An increase in quantity may signal the introduction of major players into the market, thereby making the newly emerging trends more viable.

In evaluating a candlestick pattern, volume can indicate the strength or weakness of the signal. For example, when a bullish engulfing pattern is formed with a significant volume increase, the reversal is likely to be high, as it implies increased market participation and more buying interest. On the other hand, the failure to see a volume spike may suggest that there is no conviction, therefore, making the pattern less predictable.

Trendlines, however, illustrate the direction of the market over a period of time. They act as dynamic levels of support and resistance, directing traders on where to make their entry and exit points. Trendlines are a process of connecting important price areas, including swing highs and lows, in a manner that creates a trend line indicating the direction of the trend. This line serves as a border, separating a continuation of the trend from a possible reversal.

The candlestick patterns can be further enhanced by incorporating volume analysis and trendline validation, which can be utilized to predict future trends. As an illustration, a trendline pattern established with a volume spurt is a "two-fold confirmation" of success. Such a meeting of signals enhances traders' confidence in making trades using the pattern.

False signals can also be filtered out with the help of volume and trendlines. A pattern break backed by high volume may indicate a breakout, and a pattern break backed by low volume may indicate a trap or a false signal. The difference is crucial in preventing premature ventures that may result in losses.

Additionally, volume and trendlines provide a context that helps differentiate between various market conditions. An upward trendline, supported by increasing volume, is a sign of long-term bullishness during an uptrend. Conversely, a downtrend characterized by a decreasing trend line and decreasing volume may suggest a weakening of bearish pressure, which could be a signal of a potential reversal.

In fact, traders can use platform tools to configure volume indicators and trendlines effectively. The services of TradingView and MetaTrader offer options that enable traders to superimpose volume data on their graphs and draw trendlines accurately. This graphic combination is useful for making real-time decisions, allowing traders to make quick decisions when patterns reach the validation threshold.

Ultimately, the symbiotic relationship between volume and trendlines in candlestick analysis offers a comprehensive framework for traders. Traders can enhance their decision-making process by ensuring that they are supported by volume confirmation and trendline validation, which increases the likelihood of successful trades rather than false signals. The reliability of the pattern signals is further enhanced, as the whole idea is significantly more effective in enabling the trader to move effectively in a dynamic market environment.

7

RISK MANAGEMENT AND RESILIENCE

Calculating Risk/Reward Ratios

In trading, knowledge and proper computation of risk-reward ratios are pillars of a good strategy. The process begins by understanding the core principle of risk per trade, which is closely connected to the extent of the trader's account and the quality of the candlestick pattern under discussion. It is often emphasized that one should be prudent and limit risk to 1-2 percent of the account in any one trade, as this would provide a safeguard against disastrous losses while still leaving one open to the possibility of profit.

The risk per trade is not a fixed amount, but it should be varied depending on the confidence of the trading pattern in sight. This trust stems from the past performance and reliability of the given candlestick pattern. An example is when a bullish engulfing pattern may lead a trader to adjust their risk parameter, particularly if previous experience has shown a high degree of success in a comparable market environment.

Another important part of risk/reward ratios calculations is determining the correct size of a position. This is carried out through a formulaic method, in which the risk per share, pip, or contract scales the account risk in dollar terms. The outcome provides the size of the position, ensuring the trader is not overexposed to the market. For example, a trader would buy 100 shares in a case where they risk 50 on a trade and the stop-loss distance is 0.50.

The concept of the risk-reward ratio can play a crucial role in trade decisions. The most common ratio that is frequently promoted is a 2:1 ratio, i.e., the possible reward must be at least twice the amount of risk assumed. This guideline ensures that, although fifty percent of the trades are hit, the trader still makes a profit in the long run. Such a ratio may be varied according to the trader's strategy and the market's specific conditions; however, the balance of risks and rewards must be maintained.

One way to apply these principles in practice is in a situation involving a bullish engulfing pattern. A trader can achieve a clear risk-reward situation by determining the potential target based on past highs and setting a stop-loss level below the pattern low. Traders can utilize quick-reference position sizing cheat sheets for various markets, including stocks, forex, and crypto, to perform those calculations quickly and accurately.

In addition, fractional sizing may be required due to the volatility of the asset under consideration, especially when dealing with assets such as cryptocurrencies, whose price movements can be more extreme. In this case, the changing position size to reflect high volatility is useful in ensuring continuity in risk management.

Finally, these are not only numbers but also a disciplined approach to trading that requires effectiveness in calculating and managing risk-reward ratios. Traders can enhance their decision-making process by adhering to these principles and continually refining their methods in response to market feedback, thereby minimizing emotional trading and achieving improved overall performance. The visibility provided by knowledge of these ratios will enable traders to trade with greater assurance and accuracy in the complex market world.

Position Sizing Strategies

Position sizing is important to trading and risk management. The basic rule is based on the decisions of how much of your trading capital you want to risk on a single trade. It is both a capital preservation strategy and a strategy for maximizing gain potential. One principle that is frequently suggested is the 1-2% rule of risk. This implies that you should not have more than 1-2 percent of your total account balance at risk whenever doing any given trade. The strategy enables you to control any losses and maintain them at a reasonable level so that a handful of bad trades do not drain your capital as a trader.

The quality of the candlestick setup is closely associated with position sizing. A relatively larger position size will accompany a more confident belief in a trend, whereas a more conservative stance should accompany a less confident belief. An example would be a clear bullish engulfing pattern could indicate a bigger position than one with less clarity or confirmation. Position size is calculated by dividing the dollar amount you are willing to risk by the risk per share, per pip, or per contract. The formula ensures that the position size aligns with your risk and the individual trade structure.

Risk/reward ratio is another very important element of position sizing. A trade must be evaluated as long as it has a favorable risk-reward ratio, which is typically 2:1 or greater. This is because the reward you are receiving is less compared to the amount of risk you are taking. This principle ensures that, although only a small percentage of trades may turn out to be profitable, your overall trading strategy will be profitable in the long run.

Working aids, such as position sizing cheat sheets in quick reference, may be priceless. These cheat sheets provide preset position sizes for stocks, forex, and crypto, based on varying levels of stop-loss and risk tolerance. For example, when the price of your stop is set to $0.50 and you want to risk buying $50, the cheat sheet would recommend purchasing 100 shares. These tools simplify the decision-making process, particularly in rapidly evolving markets.

Fractional sizing can be utilized to mitigate the inherent volatility in the cryptocurrency market. This entails revising the size of positions to reflect the rise in risk credit associated with crypto trading. For example, traders may prefer smaller position sizes in altcoin trading due to the high volatility of these assets' price fluctuations.

Another part and parcel of position sizing is stop-loss placement. Advanced tactics include stopping beyond the pattern invalidation levels, such as below the wick of a hammer or above the top of a shooting star. This will safeguard against premature exits due to market noise. Moreover, the stops are to be adjusted to the volatility of assets and the market environment, utilizing tools such as the Average True Range (ATR) to adjust the stops in volatile markets.

Ultimately, risk management and potential rewards must be balanced to make informed decisions about position sizing. With these as part of your trading strategy, you will be better equipped to navigate the markets with greater confidence and discipline, and you will be able to adapt your trading strategy to meet changing market conditions more effectively.

Adapting to Volatility and Liquidity

In a volatile environment like financial trading, understanding market volatility and liquidity is crucial for adapting to and succeeding. Volatility, characterized by rapid and unpredictable price movements, can significantly impact the integrity of candlestick patterns. The wicks become longer, the bodies become larger, and there is a greater risk of pattern distortion, resulting in false breaks and sharp reversals. Traders should be attentive and identify shifts in market behavior, then adjust their strategy accordingly.

Higher volatility tends to produce longer wicks and bigger body sizes within candlestick patterns, and can therefore distort patterns and render them less trustworthy. This is particularly evident in news stories or market surprises, where trends that are usually expected to unfold in a particular way can behave erratically. An example is provided of a bullish engulfing pattern, which typically signifies an upward movement that may not yield the desired outcome in a fluctuating market.

The ease of purchase and sale without influencing the price of an asset is also a critical aspect, referred to as liquidity. Patterns may be unsuccessful in low-liquidity markets because they cannot provide reliable signals due to the lack of trading volume. This is typically observed in less liquid markets or off-peak trading periods, where thin volume may lead to exaggerated price movements or false breakouts.

Traders should revise their trading strategies to address such challenges. For example, the use of broader stop-losses can help support the broader fluctuations that occur with high volatility. Another trick is fractional position sizing, which enables traders to have lower exposure and risk under unpredictable circumstances. Additionally, one can avoid trading when there are planned news releases to minimize the impact of sudden market fluctuations.

Higher timeframes can also prove useful in filtering out the noise of fast-moving markets. Traders will be able to observe long-term patterns, giving them a better understanding to mitigate the chances of responding to short-term fluctuations. The reliability of trades can also be enhanced by waiting for multi-candle confirmations, particularly when dealing with volatile markets such as cryptocurrencies.

The primary concern in volatile and illiquid markets is effective risk management. Traders should employ actionable strategies, such as placing broader stop-losses, to avoid exits triggered by market noise. It is also recommended that pattern filters and confirmation requirements should be adjusted so that only the most trusted patterns are taken into action.

To conclude, volatility and liquidity necessitate strategic intervention to adapt to them. Traders should remain vigilant and continually adjust their strategies and risk management practices to align with the prevailing market conditions. With insights into volatility and liquidity, traders can better navigate financial market complexities and make more informed, profitable decisions. Traders can stay ahead of the competition, even in the most difficult trading environment, through strategic adjustments.

Learning from Losses

In a volatile environment like financial trading, understanding market volatility and liquidity is crucial for adapting to and succeeding. Volatility, characterized by rapid and unpredictable price movements, can significantly impact the integrity of candlestick patterns. The wicks become longer, the bodies become larger, and there is a greater risk of pattern distortion, resulting in false breaks and sharp reversals. Traders should be attentive and identify shifts in market behavior, then adjust their strategy accordingly.

Higher volatility tends to produce longer wicks and bigger body sizes within candlestick patterns, and can therefore distort patterns and render them less trustworthy. This is particularly evident in news stories or market surprises, where trends that are usually expected to unfold in a particular way can behave erratically. An example is provided of a bullish engulfing pattern, which typically signifies an upward movement that may not yield the desired outcome in a fluctuating market.

The ease of purchase and sale without influencing the price of an asset is also a critical aspect, referred to as liquidity. Patterns may be unsuccessful in low-liquidity markets because they cannot provide reliable signals due to the lack of trading volume. This is typically observed in less liquid markets or off-peak trading periods, where thin volume may lead to exaggerated price movements or false breakouts.

Traders should revise their trading strategies to address such challenges. For example, the use of broader stop-losses can help support the broader fluctuations that occur with high volatility. Another trick is fractional position sizing, which enables traders to have lower exposure and risk under unpredictable circumstances. Additionally, one can avoid trading when there are planned news releases to minimize the impact of sudden market fluctuations.

Higher timeframes can also prove useful in filtering out the noise of fast-moving markets. Traders will be able to observe long-term patterns, giving them a better understanding to mitigate the chances of responding to short-term fluctuations. The reliability of trades can also be enhanced by waiting for multi-candle confirmations, particularly when dealing with volatile markets such as cryptocurrencies.

The primary concern in volatile and illiquid markets is effective risk management. Traders should employ actionable strategies, such as placing broader stop-losses, to avoid exits triggered by market noise. It is also recommended that pattern filters and confirmation requirements should be adjusted so that only the most trusted patterns are taken into action.

To conclude, volatility and liquidity necessitate strategic intervention to adapt to them. Traders should remain vigilant and continually adjust their strategies and risk management practices to align with the prevailing market conditions. With insights into volatility and liquidity, traders can better navigate financial market complexities and make more informed, profitable decisions. Traders can stay ahead of the competition, even in the most difficult trading environment, through strategic adjustments.

8

BUILDING A PERSONALIZED TRADING PLAN

Creating a Candlestick-Driven Strategy

When developing a plan focused on candlestick patterns, it is essential to start with an understanding of the patterns' deepest capacity to mirror market psychology. The individual candlesticks serve as a record of the market's emotional condition, reflecting the battle between sellers and buyers. Before we can tap into this power, we must first come to grips with the basic components of candlestick anatomy: the body, wicks, and their implications on market sentiment.

The main part of the candlestick is the essence of the price change in the selected period. A long body reflects high buying pressure or selling pressure hence momentum in the direction of the body. Short bodies, on the other hand, reflect periods of indecision or consolidation where neither the buyer nor the seller has strong authority. The wicks, or shadows, provide hints about the volatility and price extremes witnessed during the period. Long wicks may indicate rejection zones where the price made and failed to maintain specific levels, and they frequently indicate possible reversals or extensions.

To transform such observations into a coherent strategy, a trader must select candlestick patterns that best align with their trading habits and risk tolerance. Examples of such patterns include the Bullish Engulfing and the Hammer, which are usually preferred because they are reliable at predicting reversals. The Bullish Engulfing pattern consists of a small bearish candle, followed by a larger bullish candle that completely covers the previous one, indicating a significant change in momentum from sellers to buyers. The Hammer, with a small body and a long lower wick, suggests a bottoming and a rally by buyers after the sellers had forced the price down.

The confirmation of indicators should be integrated with these patterns in the creation of a strategy. Moving averages and volume analysis can serve as a valuable validation tool. An Engulfing pattern going up, such as a Bullish Engulfing, which appears on a rising 50-day moving average, has more weight and thus corresponds to longer-term bullish patterns. Likewise, when a spike in volume accompanies a Hammer pattern, it indicates that an underlying conviction is driving the move, which enhances the reliability of the pattern.

Any sound trading strategy is based on risk management. It is essential to put specific entry and exit points, as well as stop losses. When the engulfing pattern is Bullish, an entry can be made high above the high of the engulfing candle, and a stop loss can be set low beneath the low of the engulfing candle. The risk-reward ratio must be positive; it is generally advisable to have a minimum ratio of 2:1 to ensure that any gains realized significantly outweigh the risks.

Lastly, it is necessary to appraise and modify continually. Market changes, and so does the strategy. A trading journal where patterns, results, and emotions are recorded can help improve technique and inform corrective actions based on successes and failures. This is a great discipline that keeps a trader in line and, in fact, well-versed with what is happening in the market, allowing them to move around with clarity and confidence.

Incorporating Daily Routines

When it comes to trading, with all actions potentially hinging on the fine details and the time of the day, making a daily routine is not a recommendation, but a necessity. Having a systematic routine is the foundation of successful trading, as it provides a structure that helps achieve clarity of mind and strategy. It is upon these day-to-day rituals that traders are able to exercise the discipline required to sail across the turbulent waters of the market.

Every day, it begins with the preparation phase, a crucial time when traders focus on the market's needs. It involves reviewing the trades made the previous day, examining the achievements and losses, and setting clear goals for the day ahead. Through this reflective practice, traders develop a reservoir of knowledge that they utilize in future decision-making processes, and thus every action becomes informed by experience and learning.

With the opening of the market, attention is paid to observation and analysis. Traders carefully go over charts and recognize possible patterns and setups that are consistent with their trading strategy. It is a time of heightened awareness, and the ability to distinguish between market noise and meaningful signals is crucial. This is where the art of pattern recognition is developed, allowing traders to make informed decisions when presented with an opportunity.

It is also essential to incorporate breaks into the trading routine. These are the periods that offer the much-needed relief from the heavy focus required by market analysis, preventing burnout and cognitive fatigue. These breaks may include a few minutes of physical exercise or mindfulness practices by traders, which help them restructure their state of mind and become more focused when they return to the screens.

As the day progresses in the trading session, the value of being flexible becomes increasingly apparent. Markets are dynamic, and the ability to adapt strategies to changing conditions is very important. Traders should be alert and prepared to redefine their positions, ready to adjust when the time comes. This flexibility is supported by the fact that it has a routine that entails frequent review and amendment of strategies to ensure that traders are aligned with their overall objectives.

Another critical stage in the routine is the end of the trading day. It is a period of reflection and recording, and traders take their experiences and transform them into actionable knowledge. Keeping a trading journal is a practice that enables traders to note down their impressions, trades, and emotional reactions. This not only helps in determining trends in behavior and performance but also serves as a means of continual improvement.

Ultimately, day-to-day trading practice fosters a disciplined approach to performance and well-being. Through a systematic structure, traders will be in a position not only to face the technical aspects of the market, but they will also be prepared to handle the psychological aspects of trading. It is this all-round approach, combining analysis with self-care, that makes trading a worthwhile and lasting pursuit, one to be enjoyed.

Using Trading Plan Templates

When it comes to trading, being organized is crucial for navigating market complexities. A trading plan template is one of the most effective tools for achieving this goal. Such templates are elaborate tools that help traders establish their strategies, goals, and discipline throughout the entire trading process.

A trading plan template serves as a roadmap, outlining all aspects of the trading process. It begins with a clear statement of the strategy, which serves as the foundation of a winning trading plan. This assertion clarifies what the trader aims to achieve and the specific mechanisms that will be employed to accomplish this. It also incorporates the types of markets to be traded, the time periods the trader will target, and the specific patterns or arrangements the trader will observe.

Pattern identification criteria are the next important element of a trading plan template. This section describes the specific candlestick patterns the trader will use as trade entry and exit signals. Through a clear definition of these patterns, traders can eliminate guesswork and make fewer emotional decisions. Both patterns are accompanied by a checklist that features entry and exit rules, placement of stop-loss, and target-setting strategies. Such a careful strategy will prepare traders to work effectively in various market conditions and act with confidence.

Another important component included in trading plan templates is risk management. This section of the template provides a summary of how the trader approaches risk management, including setting a maximum loss per trade, determining position sizes, and utilizing stop-loss orders to manage risk effectively. With these rules, traders will be able to secure their capital and avoid losses, even in the unstable market.

Review and adaptation are also important to a trading plan template. A special section of the review process will motivate traders to review their performance on a timely basis. This includes analyzing trades, identifying what has worked and what has not, and making necessary changes to the plan. A constant improvement loop is the key to long-term success, as it enables traders to learn from their experiences and refine their strategies over time.

Furthermore, trading plan templates often require handy items such as pre-trading setup checklists and post-trading procedures. These instruments help traders remain consistent in their strategy; therefore, they are well-equipped both before entering the market and after trading. Traders can make it a routine and discipline themselves, and concentrate more.

Additionally, several trading plan templates allow customization of settings to individual preferences and trading styles. This customization will enable traders to adjust alert sensitivities, customize timeframes, and utilize asset filters that align with their distinct trading strategies. This type of customization is crucial for minimizing the number of false alarms and ensuring that alerts are tailored to the trader's specific objectives.

Essentially, trading plan templates involve creating organized and disciplined trading strategies. These templates provide a clear guideline that helps traders make informed decisions, manage risks properly, and continuously optimize their strategies. Through these tools, traders can enhance their confidence, manage their emotional trading, and improve their chances of success in the fast-paced world of financial markets.

Ongoing Review and Adjustment

Flexibility is an essential aspect in the world of trade, and this ability separates experienced traders from those who are new. The active nature of financial markets necessitates continuous monitoring and the ability to adjust approaches in response to changing conditions. This continuous review and realignment process is not only a reactionary solution but also an initiative to achieve long-term success in trading.

A key aspect of this process is the fact that there is no infallibility in trading strategies. The markets are influenced by a range of factors, including macroeconomic variables and geopolitical events, whose effects can alter market dynamics in unpredictable ways. The traders should thus develop a culture of consistently revising their strategies to identify areas for improvement, as well as to ensure they are aligned with prevailing market conditions.

The primary aspect of this ongoing review process is the meticulous maintenance of a trading journal. This journal is a collection of trades, encapsulating the entry and exit points, the reasons that led to the trade, and the outcomes. Creating an organized list of these factors allows traders to analyse their work in retrospect with an eye to detecting patterns and biases that could have affected their performance. This reflection exercise is not only useful in improving self-awareness but also enables the researcher to have empirical evidence to make future trading decisions.

Additionally, the trading journal will help traders identify their common errors and develop strategies to avoid them. For example, when a trader consistently incurs losses due to premature exits, they may investigate methods for placing a more effective stop-loss order or learn to wait until a trade has fulfilled its potential. These are the kind of insights that you gain based on historical performance, which are priceless in perfecting trading methodologies.

Beyond personal analysis, it is possible to explore trading communities to gain additional perspectives and a deeper understanding. Webinars, mentorship, and forums provide traders with the opportunity to exchange experiences and strategies, fostering a collaborative learning environment. Such exchanges may expose traders to new strategies and tools that they would not have encountered on their own, thereby expanding their strategic range.

Technology is also crucial in the review and readjustment process. State-of-the-art trading platforms offer a wealth of analytical tools and indicators that can significantly enhance a trader's ability to analyze the market landscape and evaluate the performance of a strategy. Through these tools, traders can conduct more advanced analyses, such as testing their strategies on a historical basis, to ensure their effectiveness. This fact-based strategy ensures that changes are not undertaken based on feelings, but rather on quantitative data.

Additionally, traders must be aware of broader market trends and developments. The announcements of economic reports, interest rates, and geopolitical events may all have significant effects on market volatility and price change. By remaining aware of these, traders can anticipate the potential changes that may occur in the market and adjust their plans accordingly.

Ultimately, the ability to develop is the key to successful trading. Markets are ever-changing, and strategies that work today might not necessarily work tomorrow. Traders can achieve this by ensuring they invest in a process of continuous review and adaptation, so as not only to survive in the dynamic environment of the financial markets, but also to thrive. It is this dedication to constant betterment that makes trading more of a speculative enterprise than a disciplined one, as it is able to produce consistent results over time.

9

REAL-WORLD APPLICATION ACROSS MARKETS

Pattern Adaptation for Stocks, Forex, and Crypto

The flexibility of candlestick patterns in the financial markets of stocks, forex, and cryptocurrencies is crucial for traders who want to leverage market dynamics. The asset classes have distinct issues and opportunities that require a sophisticated appreciation of candlestick applications. Adaptation of patterns in these different environments will occur through the identification of the nature of each market, which may significantly impact the consistency and interpretation of candlestick signals.

The systematic trading hours and regulations that govern stock markets tend to exhibit patterns that influence market dynamics, often with a tendency to open and close. Stock market traders need to consider the effects of overnight news and pre-market activity that might create gaps, which can interfere with pattern building. Candlestick patterns should be considered in the context of predictable stock market cycles, such as earnings seasons and quarterly reports. For example, a bullish engulfing pattern may be more effective following a high-earnings report, as it can confirm the buying interest.

Conversely, the forex market operates 24/7, five days a week, with the global economy and geopolitics always in motion. This is an ongoing cycle, and this introduces another set of challenges in pattern recognition. The high liquidity and volatility of the forex market imply that patterns can be generated and registered quickly; therefore, a trader may need to use longer timeframes to filter out noise. Forex traders should be able to identify patterns in the relationship between currency pairs and the policies of central banks, which can have a significant influence on price fluctuations. A pin bar pattern may exist, carrying more weight when accompanied by a central bank announcement or the release of a significant economic indicator.

Cryptocurrencies are relatively new compared to stocks and forex, and they operate in a 24/7 decentralized marketplace. No centralized control can cause overstated price movements and pattern shaping due to the influence of market sentiment. This means that crypto traders should be especially wary of so-called fake outs, or fake breakouts or breakdowns, given that the market is prone to speculative actions and low liquidity in some coins. Cryptocurrency volatility also means that traders need to adjust their pattern recognition parameters, typically seeking multi-candle confirmation or a volume explosion to confirm the strength of a pattern.

Making candlestick patterns applicable to these different asset classes does not mean just identifying the development of a pattern, but rather gathering appropriate context to which the pattern is applied. Traders should refine their strategy by taking into account aspects such as market liquidity, the day of the week, and external economic factors. This flexibility does not merely mean the ability to identify patterns on a case-by-case basis, but to incorporate them into a larger trading strategy that considers the unique dynamics of a particular market. In this way, traders will be able to make more informed decisions and ultimately increase their chances of success in the diverse financial trading environment.

Timing Trades for Optimal Success

Knowing the market's beat is a skill that every trader seeking success can learn. The ability to predict when to join or exit a trade can play a significant role in the results, potentially turning potential losses into gains. Timing trades is a sophisticated science that requires a solid understanding of market dynamics, the reliability of the pattern, and the role played by non-market factors, such as news and trading sessions.

To begin learning how to trade the time, it is essential to understand how various times of the day and week can impact market activity. Close and open market time conditions are critical, as they typically determine the direction and volatility of trading. An example is the U.S. stock market, whose power hour occurs after opening, as it is viewed as the time when most orders are placed by investors who have just read the news and analysis that occurred overnight. On the other hand, activity levels tend to be low during the lunch lull, which results in less volatility and fewer trading opportunities.

In the forex market, the overlap between the London and New York sessions is a period of high liquidity and volatility, making it an opportune time for trading. The overlap provides trading leeway for traders to take advantage of the increased activity and possibly more dependable pattern developments. The nature of these market dynamics highlights the importance of understanding the temporal aspects of trading, as they can significantly influence the credibility of candlestick patterns.

Another factor influencing the timing of the trade is the weekends and holidays, particularly in the cryptocurrency and foreign exchange markets. Liquidity is likely to become thin in such periods, leading to the threat of fake outs and unstable price changes. Weekends may be particularly hazardous for crypto traders because the markets are open 24/7, resulting in erratic highs and lows that are further exacerbated by the absence of institutional investors.

These temporal changes must be addressed strategically. Traders should develop a timing cheat sheet that indicates the optimal time to trade specific assets. This guide will enable traders to avoid wasting time when volume is low and take advantage of moments when patterns are more likely to be effective. Additionally, the awareness of the specifics of overlaps in the sessions and the opening of the markets can provide clues about when the patterns will show consistently.

Moreover, news events play a very important role in timing trades. Announcements on the market, such as economic reports or corporate earnings, can cause significant shifts in the market. Traders must be vigilant in observing such events and evaluating the potential consequences for their trading strategies. One can reduce the risk of unexpected volatility and preserve capital by avoiding trades during times of major news releases.

Finally, the optimal success of timing trades cannot be achieved solely through an understanding of patterns but also requires a thorough knowledge of market cycles and other external factors. Traders can maximize their likelihood of successful trades by ensuring that trading practice is consistent with the normal operation of the market and that they take note of the factors that influence the reliability of the pattern. It is a combination of disciplined risk management and constant learning that is the backbone of a successful trading practice.

Platform-Specific Execution Examples

It requires a sharp insight into the specifics of each platform to navigate the complex world of trading across all platforms. In the stock trading industry, there are various stock trading systems, such as Think or swim, that provide tools to optimize the trading experience. Among the most prominent characteristics is the use of bracket orders, which allow traders to set both a profit target and a stop-loss, thereby helping to control and manage risks and returns. This feature is essential for traders of large-cap stocks, where price fluctuations may be more predictable but still require accurate control to generate profits.

In the meantime, forex trading via software such as MetaTrader introduces its own tool set, designed to handle the swifter and more turbulent currency markets.

The pending orders option in MetaTrader is ideal, as it enables traders to develop accurate entry points. This is especially useful in forex, where factors such as tight spreads and sudden news moves can open opportunities that must be pursued as soon as possible with a strategic move. The platform's trailing stop feature also helps mitigate risk as a trade is heading in the right direction, and the stop-loss will automatically adjust to market movements.

TradingView is a powerful tool in the crypto world, particularly in the field of trading the volatile aspects of the crypto market. Its alert system is such a potent tool that traders do not have to constantly watch the charts, only to be informed about market movements. This comes in handy, especially when monitoring the highly unstable price movements of top cryptocurrencies, such as BTC/USD. With the alerts, traders can respond quickly to market changes, allowing them to act on opportunities as they arise.

The unique tools in each platform enable certain trading strategies that can be most effectively applied to a specific asset class. For example, with stocks, the trade journaling tool in Thinkorswim can be used to track trading patterns and results, allowing traders to refine their strategies over time. Conversely, the order templates provided by MetaTrader are flexible, enabling forex traders to easily reproduce successful trades and adapt them to the fast-paced currency markets.

Moreover, the ability to adapt to live trade adjustments is a crucial skill across all platforms. It could involve relocating a stop once the initial profit target has been met or exiting a position to ensure a profit while still having room to profit further. Every operation will demand a keen approach to the market environment and the tools available. As is the case with the stock market, pre-market gaps present special challenges, which necessitate the use of a strategic stop to prevent being trapped in adverse moves.

Overall, both trading platforms provide a collection of trading tools that can be applied to trading stocks, forex, or cryptocurrencies. The ability to use these tools not only increases the efficiency of the trade but also enables traders to make informed choices in real-time. Through platform-specific functions, traders will be able to manage risks more effectively and design strategies that suit the dynamic environment of each market. Such flexibility is essential for achieving consistency in the multifaceted world of trading.

Case Studies of Successful Trades

When it comes to the trading market, the true skill of the trade is to navigate the intricate world of financial markets with accuracy and confidence. This part delves into the intricate dynamics of winning trades, examining the art and science behind this type of trade. All of the case studies serve as a testament to the strength of candlestick patterns and how they can be utilized to identify lucrative opportunities under varying market conditions.

Consider a trader who has learned through experience the rise and fall of the market cycles and who is aware of the subtlety of the candlesticks in a chart. This merchant has mastered the skill of identifying trends amidst confusion and reducing potential market noise into a single signal. In one instance, a bullish engulfing pattern is visible on the chart of a major tech company. The trader is an expert in the anatomy of candlesticks and is the one who saw the engulfing pattern as an indication of a probable reversal. With this understanding, the trader waits until there is confirmation, which occurs when the consequent candle closes higher than the high of the engulfing pattern. This patience will pay off when the stock takes off and the trader is justified in his disciplined pattern recognition strategy.

The forex market, characterized by volatility and high fluctuations, presents an entirely different challenge in another situation. In this case, a trader identifies a hammer at the bottom of a down trend in the EUR/USD currency pair. Recognizing the psychological struggles of buyers and sellers, the trader can interpret the long lower wick as an indicator of buyer support. Entering a long position is not easy; it is well-planned, and the risk is managed meticulously, so that the stop-loss is set just below the wick. When the currency pair reverses, the trade is successful and demonstrates the trader's skill in handling forex volatility through the use of candlestick knowledge.

Another canvas on which candlestick skills can be mastered is cryptocurrency markets, whose own volatility and trading behaviour are peculiar. A shrewd trader sees what appears on the Bitcoin chart as a bullish sign: a morning star pattern. The trader is extremely conscious of how volume is a validating element in crypto trades. With the completion of the morning star, the volume of trading increases, which confirms the validity of the pattern. A trader enters the market, showing confidence, and sets a target that is determined by past resistance levels. The trade is executed to achieve a positive outcome, which supports the trader in integrating the concepts of price action and volume analysis.

These case studies highlight the effectiveness and utility of candlestick patterns in various markets. They emphasize the context, such as the direction and volume of the trend, to enhance the reliability of the patterns. Additionally, they emphasize the importance of risk management in conserving capital and maximizing returns. Every winning trade involves a perfect result of disciplined analysis, strategic entry, and wise exit.

These examples help traders develop a critical insight into patterns, patience to wait until it confirms, and the flexibility to adjust their strategies to the individuality of a particular market. Learning to use candlestick patterns is an ongoing process of learning and adjustment, and every trade helps to understand the market's dynamics further. The more traders learn and perfect their craft, the more they are able to see opportunities clearly and confidently as they bring the art of candlestick analysis to life and become successful traders.

10

ADVANCED TECHNIQUES FOR MASTERY

Multi-Candle Patterns and Their Uses

The ability to interpret the complexities of a multi-candle pattern in the dynamic world of financial markets can go a long way in helping traders foresee market actions. These formations, which represent groups of candlesticks, present a comprehensive picture of market sentiment, as they capture the psychology of buyers and sellers over a specific time frame. Multi-candle patterns, unlike single candlestick patterns, provide a broader picture that illustrates trends, reversals, and continuations, which can be easily used as guiding features in making informed trading decisions.

The multi-candle patterns are simply the stories of the market's psychology and summaries of the battle within the market between bullish and bearish moods. Every pattern tells a story; a "Three-Line Strike" pattern, consisting of four candles, indicates that the trend is well-supported after a short, unsuccessful reversal. This trend can be seen as an unsuccessful effort by one party to reverse the trend, only to be overwhelmed by the mainstream mood, thus confirming the trend direction.

The other interesting multi-candle formation is the so-called Abandoned Baby, not particularly common, but it is a strong reversal signal. The formation of this pattern is based on the presence of a gap between candles, indicating a rapid change in market sentiment. The Abandoned Baby is usually seen as the culmination of a long line and indicates a possible reversal. The psychological meaning of this is that the market has exhausted its current trend and is about to switch to the other end, and in many cases, traders are taken unawares.

Another type of multi-candle formation is the Stick Sandwich pattern, which illustrates the tug-of-war between buyers and sellers. It is defined by two bearish candles surrounding a bullish candle, indicating some temporary stagnation in a down trend. This trend indicates that sellers have been on the winning side, but buyers are starting to build strength, which may cause the trend to reverse or continue with the bullish momentum as long as the following candles follow suit.

All these patterns, although individual in their formation, share one commonality: they provide valuable insights into market dynamics. They provide traders with insight into future price trends, enabling them to plan effectively. The most important thing to note about using these patterns is that they must be confirmed; that is, one has to wait until the next candle closes in the expected direction, thus minimizing false alarms.

Additionally, multi-candle patterns are not effective as isolated indicators; their maximum effectiveness is achieved when they are combined with trend analysis, volume indicators, and other technical indicators. This is a systematic method that improves a trader's ability to confirm signals and make trades with greater confidence. For example, volume analysis can be used in conjunction with multi-candle patterns to verify the intensity of a breakout or the probability of a failed pattern, thereby optimizing entry and exit techniques.

Essentially, learning to read multi-candle patterns equips the trader with a robust toolkit to navigate the dynamics of financial markets. Through these patterns, traders will be better equipped to interpret market sentiment in terms of its rise and fall, and as such, they will be able to pinpoint high-probability setups that align with their strategies. Such information is not only able to help mitigate trading risks, but also to increase the possibility of regularly achieving high profits. Such insights are invaluable for the long-term success of trading in a constantly changing world.

Pattern Journaling for Continuous Improvement

Pattern journaling is a crucial aspect of the trades practiced by traders seeking to achieve self-improvement and mastery over their trading. Through their careful records of every trade, traders are able to turn their lives into a wealth of learning, noticing all the little details that bring their triumphs and defeats. This is not a process of data gathering, but a reflective process that improves trading acumen and decision-making processes.

The journaling process begins with a comprehensive entry for every single trade setup, covering market conditions, detected patterns, entry and exit points, and the trade's results. Such detailed logging is a source of information that, over time, can give an overview of trends in trades and their reactions in the market. By periodically reviewing such data, traders will know which pattern is most effective under these conditions and optimize their strategies to include high-probability setups.

Pattern journaling is not only a reflection of a trader's psychological state, but it is also a technical tool. Traders can begin to recognize the impact of their mental state on their trading decisions by recording their emotions in the moments before and after trades, such as confidence, anxiety, and impulsiveness. This realization plays a vital role in developing the discipline necessary to execute trading plans effectively and avoid emotional traps that lead to suboptimal decision-making.

Additionally, journaling helps traders become more scientific in their trading. Seeing every trade as an experiment allows traders to make speculations about how the market will behave, then test their hypotheses by making actual trades and examining the results to either confirm or refine their strategies. Hypothesis testing and analysis, as an iterative process, possess characteristics that are crucial to success in the dynamic trading world, including a state of constant learning and continuous adjustment.

Accountability is also made possible by pattern journaling. By recording their trades, they leave a record that they can provide to mentors or peers to receive feedback. Such an external check may be quite insightful, as a more seasoned trader may be able to detect certain biases or mistakes that the trader has missed. This collaborative learning fosters faster development and encourages openness and honesty about personal trading activities.

Besides personal development, pattern journaling helps traders survive in the market during volatile situations. Through the documentation of previous trading, traders can compile a database of market tendencies, learning to detect and adjust to new circumstances. This flexibility is essential in unstable markets, where decisions must be made quickly in most cases. The availability of a well-documented history will enable traders to be more confident about the pitfalls to avoid and the opportunities to exploit.

Ultimately, pattern journaling is not merely a record-keeping process but a strategic tool that enables traders to transform data into actionable insights. By instilling a culture of reflection and analysis, traders can continually refine their strategies, develop psychological resilience, and enhance their overall trading performance. By doing so, pattern journaling can become an indispensable addition to the trader's toolkit, leading to a never-ending cycle of improvement and preparing the way for mastering trading.

Leveraging Community Feedback

When it comes to trading, particularly in mastering candlestick patterns, the feedback and insights of a group can be a decisive factor in refining approaches and enhancing decision-making. Interaction with other traders is a vibrant area of experience exchange, where one can learn from the successes and failures of other traders, as well as stay informed about market trends and innovations. This community style not only adds value to individual knowledge but also creates a conducive atmosphere in which traders can develop collectively.

The number of trading communities available online is extremely high, and websites like Discord, Reddit, and Fin Twit are popular platforms for communication. Such areas provide real-time feedback, allowing traders to negotiate potential trades, analyze chart patterns, and discuss market movements. Exposure to diverse views and trading styles can significantly enhance the interpretation of candlestick patterns for traders who are part of these communities. Nevertheless, one must be careful of these platforms. Among the valuable information, we may also find misguided information and guidance from less experienced or unproven sources. That is why traders need to learn to differentiate between credible mentors and valuable feedback from noise.

To maximize the benefits of community feedback, traders should adopt best practices for sharing and receiving critiques. This is achieved by having clear annotations on charts and asking specific questions that stimulate constructive feedback. By posing specific questions, traders can receive tailored advice relevant to their doubts or concerns. Additionally, involvement in community challenges, pattern contests, or review sessions may also help develop these skills. These activities can not only provide practical experience but also offer a chance to be recognized and learn from experienced traders.

It can also be beneficial to establish a system of accountability partners within these communities. Such partners can provide consistent feedback to ensure discipline and compliance with trading plans. Additionally, the ability to engage in smaller and more focused study groups may provide a more intimate learning experience, allowing for in-depth analysis and discussion, and yielding more profound insights and personal connections.

Community feedback is priceless, but one needs to be critical and analytical in order to derive meaningful insights. Traders should always verify the advice against their own research and analysis. This is a two-fold strategy, so that trading decisions are made based on information, not on mere opinion. In addition, traders must exercise caution when dealing with traders labeled as gurus who sell their signals or offer guaranteed returns, as such assurances are often not substantiated.

Ultimately, community feedback can be highly beneficial to any trader seeking to master the application of candlestick patterns. It offers an immense amount of knowledge and varied opinions, none of which are insignificant in helping one cope with the intricacies of the trading environment. Through active involvement in these communities and critical thinking, traders are positioned to sharpen their skills, make more informed choices, and ultimately achieve greater success in their trading endeavors. When effectively utilized, the wisdom of a collective can catalyze personal development and the art of candlestick trading.

Avoiding Burnout and Maintaining Focus

The menace of burnout is enormous to many traders in the unrelenting quest to master the art of trading. The insatiable nature of the candlestick patterns can overpower one as one tries to navigate the complex world of candlestick patterns. To achieve a sustainable pace, it is essential to incorporate strategies that not only keep the mind sharp but also promote a balanced lifestyle.

The first key approach to avoiding burnout is to develop a proper routine that includes taking breaks. Like markets, there are good and bad times, so a trader should also have time for rest. This can be achieved by arranging frequent screen time breaks to alleviate the mental strain of continuous chart analysis. Taking a break away from the screen, even for a few minutes, can rejuvenate the mind and enhance concentration when returning to market analysis.

An additional useful technique is to switch between studying, practicing, and live trading. Not only does this rotation diversify the mental load, but it also expands the trader's skill base, making them more adaptable in different market conditions. The strategy will make sure that there is no repetitive or excessive strain in any part of the trading process.

Along with these structural strategies, it is necessary to approach trading holistically. This entails incorporating mindfulness and exercise into everyday life.

Practices such as meditation or yoga can substantially improve mental clarity and lower stress levels. Exercises, whether a brisk walk or a full workout, help release endorphins, which are natural stress-relievers. Traders can enhance their mental acuity and emotional resilience by maintaining good physical health.

Another crucial aspect that can be achieved by community support is maintaining motivation and focus. Interacting with other traders via a forum or social media channel is one way of having peer check-ins and support. Such exchanges may offer a fresh perspective and alleviate feelings of loneliness, while also fostering a stronger sense of belonging within the trading community.

Moreover, lifelong learning must be part of the way of life of any trader. Lifelong learning ensures that the mind remains well-flexed and receptive to new strategies and market trends. By regularly checking new and old patterns, updating journals with lessons from triumphs and failures, and engaging in more in-depth study materials (such as books, webinars, and podcasts), it is possible to achieve continuous improvement and avoid stagnation.

Through such measures, traders will be able to develop a sustainable and concentrated trading practice. The key is to recognize the symptoms of burnout before they escalate and address them proactively. By maintaining a moderate approach to balancing the mind and body, traders can remain engaged in the markets and perform at their best.

11

UTILIZING TECHNOLOGY FOR ENHANCED TRADING

Automated Pattern Recognition Tools

Automated pattern recognition tools have become central partners to traders in the world of candlestick charting, offering a convenient and accurate combination that is often lacking in manual chart analysis. These platforms are built to integrate with TradingView, MetaTrader, and Thinkorswim, utilizing advanced algorithms to scan markets for candlestick patterns. This enables traders to receive timely alerts and make informed decisions.

The nature of these tools is that they can process large volumes of information in real-time and identify possible trading signals that a human eye cannot detect, particularly in high-volatility markets. This is especially useful when dealing with traders who trade in various asset classes, such as stocks, forex, and cryptocurrencies, because the amount of data may be overwhelming. These tools simplify the trading process by automating the pattern recognition process, allowing traders to focus on strategy and execution, rather than the finer details of chart analysis.

Nonetheless, there are some limitations to the usefulness of automated pattern recognition. These tools are skillful at identifying patterns, although not flawless. False positives can also occur when using these algorithms, especially in markets with low liquidity or high volatility. An example is that a pattern found in a turbulent market may not be as valid as it would be in a more tranquil market. Thus, these tools are typically recommended to traders as an additional resource to supplement manual analysis and verify signals.

One of the most important characteristics of automated pattern recognition tools is their ability to be customized, which enhances their effectiveness. Traders can generally customize the sensitivity of alerts, change time limits, and filter assets according to their unique trading strategies. This customization is useful in minimizing the noise of false signals, making the alerts received in the field relevant to the individual trader's approach and market orientation.

Even with their high-tech abilities, they are not meant to replace the sophisticated skills and knowledge of experienced professionals in market conditions. Traders are advised to develop a workflow that incorporates both automated signaling and manual confirmation to ensure optimal trading outcomes. This could include rechecking the trend, volume, and market in general before taking an alert. This type of balanced strategy not only reduces the chance of receiving a false signal but also helps a trader trust their choices.

Comparing the two systems — manual and automated pattern spotting —both have their own benefits. Manual analysis is slower, but it provides a better understanding of the background and insight into market dynamics. Automated tools, on the other hand, are fast and efficient, making them ideal for traders who need to track multiple markets simultaneously. An integrated methodology is typically the most effective, as it leverages the strengths of both approaches.

Ultimately, when automated pattern recognition tools are integrated into a trader's arsenal, they can significantly enhance their analytical capabilities. These tools make traders less prone to the intricacies of candlestick charting, allowing them to make more informed and confident trading decisions by providing faster and more precise insights into the chart.

Backtesting Without Coding

Backtesting is a crucial practice in the world of trading, as it enables traders to test the effectiveness of their strategies without risking real money. The beauty of backtesting is that it enables traders to predict the outcome of a trade using historical data, thereby determining the feasibility of their strategies. Nevertheless, the technical aspect of coding is a daunting challenge to most. Alas, a viable solution to this problem is provided by manual backtesting, which can be performed by any trader, regardless of their familiarity with coding languages.

This is achieved by first selecting the asset and timeframe that align with the trader's objective. When selected, the trader reviews historical data and carefully identifies every occurrence of the pattern they want to test. This manual method, despite its time-intensive nature, creates a better insight into the market behavior and subtleties that automated mechanisms can miss.

Recent documentation of the details of every trade is also a major feature of manual backtesting. This involves recording the entry and exit points, the circumstances that led to the trade, the result, and indicators that support it. Maintaining a detailed log is essential because it enables an in-depth analysis of how the pattern has performed over time. The sample backtest log template can be useful in this respect, as it will ensure consistent and accurate data recording.

After compiling the data, traders will be able to analyze the results. The most important indicators include win rate, average return, drawdown, and the identification of the most and least efficient setups, which provide insight into the strategy's effectiveness. This analysis can be achieved through a simple spreadsheet, allowing traders to visualize trends and identify areas for improvement.

To ensure objectivity and minimize bias, best practices should be followed during the backtesting process. Traders should be cautious of the hindsight bias, which can influence their perception of past trades. In addition, to achieve statistical significance, a sufficient number of trades must be tested, typically around 50 to 100 trades.

Pattern scorecards may also be used to augment the backtesting process with graphical reliability rankings and cheat sheets, providing quick access to information. These scorecards categorize patterns by reliability, clarity, and risk-to-reward, providing traders with a streamlined decision-making tool. During live trading, color-coded systems, such as green, yellow, and red, are used to quickly assess reliability, situational awareness, or patterns to avoid, respectively.

Manual backtesting, which does not involve any coding, is, in a sense, not a replacement for automated systems but a standalone, powerful methodology. It enables traders to delve deeply into the data, creating a nuanced understanding of market dynamics. Disciplined practice and meticulous record-keeping enable traders to refine their strategies, enhance their decision-making capabilities, and ultimately achieve more effective trading results. This practical solution demystifies the backtesting process, making it an easy-to-understand and invaluable trade tool that traders of any level can utilize.

Data-Driven Decision Making

In trading, analytical decision-making is key. The scenery is full of patterns and signals that, when properly interpreted, will result in successful trades. The problem, however, is to distinguish credible patterns from those that can cause false signals. Here is where the use of data-driven decision-making is essential.

Decision-making in trading is based on the use of statistical insights to inform decisions using data. Traders find historical data useful for supporting testing patterns, determining successful rates, and calculating average returns. This process demonstrates the likelihood of a pattern operating in other market conditions, including different time periods or asset types. For example, the success of bullish and bearish candlestick patterns can vary significantly between stocks, forex, and cryptocurrencies. Through such statistics, traders can focus on patterns that have a higher likelihood of success in the past.

The key aspect of the method is backtesting, which traders can use to replicate trades using historical data, thereby avoiding financial risks. This would help determine the strengths and weaknesses of the various patterns, providing a clearer representation of the reliability of each pattern. It involves analyzing a large number of trades to obtain a statistically significant evaluation, which can be quite time-intensive, requiring 50-100 credible trades. Backtesting will help traders optimize their strategies and focus on arrangements that consistently deliver good returns.

Furthermore, it is essential to understand the market context when making decisions based on data. Patterns do not work in an empty room; their effectiveness is often dependent on the broader market conditions. A bullish engulfing pattern, for instance, may be highly successful in a sharp upswing but ineffective in a trading market. Thus, incorporating market context, such as the strength of trends, volume, and news events, enhances the quality of pattern-based decisions.

There are also trading mechanisms, such as trading journals, that traders can use to measure their performance and refine their strategies. Capturing trades and examining the results allow traders to determine how they made a decision, identify common errors, or recognize effective strategies. This practice of reflection is not limited to data collection, but also involves the development of accountability and continuous improvement.

The addition of technology, such as automated pattern recognition tools, can also improve decision-making. These tools utilize algorithms to scan markets for potential setups and issue alerts when markets meet a predefined set of criteria. It should be noted, however, that these automated signals should be manually confirmed to prevent false positives, particularly in high-velocity or illiquid markets.

Ultimately, the issue of data-driven decision-making in trading involves integrating statistical knowledge with practical experience. It entails striking a balance between relying on experience and staying informed about prevailing market trends. In this way, traders will be able to make more informed decisions, which will minimize emotional biases and maximize the probability of successful trades. This strategy enhances trading success and fosters confidence, as decisions are informed by facts rather than intuition. Traders can act with increased accuracy and efficiency within the market by employing disciplined data-driven strategies.

Building a Pattern Scorecard

The process of creating a pattern scorecard is systematic in assessing candlestick patterns in terms of reliability, clarity, and risk/reward potential. The first step in this process is to recognize the significant patterns that traders often encounter and to evaluate these patterns systematically. The idea is to develop a tool that can rank such patterns and, simultaneously, serve as a quick reference guide for active trading.

First, it is necessary to classify patterns based on their success rates and the situations in which they can be applied. Such division can be represented in a color-coded system: green indicates high reliability, yellow indicates corresponding patterns that should be effective under certain conditions, and red indicates inherent unreliability. This type of visualization enables traders to easily identify which trends to focus on, based on their statistical performance under various market conditions.

A scorecard ought to contain an overview of entry and exit regulations of every pattern, and this must bring out the most suitable circumstances where they prosper. An example of this is the bullish engulfing pattern, which is most effective when three consecutive down candles are followed by a volume spike, indicating that a potential reversal may be underway. The presence of these subtle details will enable traders to make informed decisions on the fly.

Additionally, the pattern scorecard can be transformed into a dynamic personal trading development tool. It allows traders to create a pattern-oriented watchlist of their preferred trading patterns. That is, the scorecard will improve over time, utilizing personal insights and market experiences, which will make it more useful. The scorecard may be used to gauge performance and modify strategies. A trader may point out their three best patterns to monitor on a daily basis.

The scorecard can be further enhanced by incorporating case studies of patterns in volatile or choppy markets. The patterns in less-than-ideal conditions of pattern recognition by traders can be more effectively studied through examining real-life examples when patterns have been successful and when they have failed. This can be analyzed with visual callouts of traps, such as overlapping wicks or fake outs, which may cause false pattern recognition.

Other confirmation tools should also be promoted in the scorecard, such as volume analysis or moving averages, to augment pattern signals. An example is that a pattern may be scored better on the scorecard when it coincides with a moving average crossover or a volume explosion, making it more reliable.

Lastly, the provision of downloadable or printable templates of the scorecard is a measure that will enable traders to apply this tool with ease in their day-to-day lives. A mobile version may be particularly useful for traders who need quick access to pattern information during live trading.

In sum, the construction of a pattern scorecard is the process of developing a complex and convenient tool that improves the capacity of a trader to find his or her way through the maze of candlestick patterns. It is an ongoing system of improvement and adjustment that aims to facilitate better decision-making and ultimately achieve more successful trade results.

12

THE ART OF CONTINUOUS LEARNING

Keeping a Trading Journal

The trading journal is a valuable resource for traders, serving as a personal diary of all the trades they have made, including the reasons behind their decisions and the results. This detailed record-keeping is not just a form of documentation, but a strategic activity that enables traders to refine their strategies, learn from their trading patterns, and ultimately become more effective over time.

The trading journal is not just about making entries and exit points. It demands a holistic approach, where traders record the nature of the pattern they have seen, the market environment they were in, and how they were emotionally feeling at the time of the trade. All these factors provide people with a comprehensive perspective on every trading choice that traders have made and the market conditions that have affected their results.

Journaling helps identify trends in the market and in one's own behavior. Through continuous recording of trades, traders will be able to identify common problems they commit, such as trading based on emotions instead of logic, and not following a trading plan. This consciousness is essential for personal development, as it helps traders consciously adjust their strategies and enhance their discipline.

Additionally, a trading journal is a crucial source of post-trade analysis. Following a sequence of exchanges, examining journal entries may provide clues on which strategies are effective and which are not. This can be used to highlight the strengths of the strategy, including a high success rate in utilizing certain candlestick patterns, as well as weaknesses, such as poor performance in specific market conditions. Through these factors, traders can adjust their approaches to perform more effectively.

Traders are advised to keep a journal to stay focused and monitor their progress. For example, a trader may wish to execute a specific pattern more effectively or to remain disciplined through their established set of risk management guidelines. This enables traders to measure their progress and stay motivated by setting and regularly reviewing these goals, as well as examining their journal entries.

Moreover, the journal should be maintained properly, as it is a helpful tool for accountability. To gather outside opinions and feedback, a trader can share journal entries with a mentor or a trading community, which can further enhance their learning process. This is done not only to encourage growth but also to create a sense of community and solidarity among traders.

A trading journal has the power to transform trading from an unstructured, tumultuous effort into what it can be. By keeping accurate records and analyzing them regularly, traders can gain a deeper understanding of their trading style and make more informed decisions. This transparency is essential for fostering trust and stability in the face of market volatility.

Simply put, having a trading journal is not merely a process of recording trades; it is a process of self-improvement and discipline. It enables traders to learn from both successes and failures, developing a greater insight into the markets and themselves. The more skillfully traders learn to interpret their journal entries, the more effective their strategies, the less they involve emotional trading, and the more successful they are in their trading activities.

Staying Sharp with Pattern Drills

In the complex business of candlestick trading, it is the sharpness of the edge that is most important to success. This acuity is refined through the laborious training of pattern drills, an exercise that is not only time-tested but also indispensable to any trader who wants to achieve excellence. Pattern recognition is an art, similar to any other art form, and it requires consistent and intensive training to become proficient and confident in real trading situations.

Pattern drills form the foundation of this practice, as they provide traders with the opportunity to train in a controlled setting. Such exercises replicate the pressure of a real-life market situation, where traders must respond promptly and accurately to emerging patterns. The game aims to replicate the disorder of live trading, where indicators are often lost in market noise and overlap. Through these exercises, traders become familiar with the legitimate patterns within the noise and are better placed to make quick and informed choices.

To remain alert, it is essential to incorporate a wide range of charts and various timeframes into these exercises. This variety ensures that traders are well-equipped to handle the various market conditions they may encounter. A one-minute forex chart is a challenge compared to a daily stock chart or a volatile cryptocurrency market. Every situation demands a certain strategy and mindset, which the drills help one develop. Having the answer keys and a rationale behind every exercise improves the learning process, giving the traders a better insight into the correct and incorrect identifications.

Additionally, pattern drills focus not only on recognition but also on timing. The Traders are then encouraged to trade under time constraints, which mimics the rush to make decisions in a live market. This element of the exercises is essential, as it develops the trader's ability to act decisively under pressure, which is incredibly important when trading with actual money on the line.

Another necessary part of being sharp is tracking the progress. Traders can maintain a scorecard and progress log, setting tangible goals to achieve. These applications enable traders to view their average time per pattern and accuracy percentage, providing them with concrete metrics to track their progress. Such a data-based method not only creates a desire to improve but also fosters a sense of discipline and responsibility.

Being able to identify trends in not-so-perfect situations is a quality of a good trader. Pattern recognition in practice: The practical use of pattern recognition frequently needs to contend with messy market conditions, in which textbook-optimal patterns are rare occurrences. Exercises that focus on such situations are invaluable because they help traders refine their analysis and rely on it, even when the market is not providing clear indications.

The result of these drills is to create a trader who is not only a good pattern recognizer but also a trader who is confident in their ability to execute trades according to the patterns. The development of this confidence is achieved through repetition, analysis, and the continuous adaptation to new information. Through practicing regular pattern drills, traders are guaranteed to be prepared and able to seize opportunities whenever they arise in the dynamic nature of the financial markets.

Adapting to Market Changes

In such a dynamic financial market context, flexibility proves to be a key competitive advantage for traders who intend to remain competitive. The market dynamics are subject to ongoing change, influenced by a myriad of forces that impact economic indicators and geopolitical events. As these factors change, the behavior of market participants also changes, and this is readily apparent in the candlestick chart patterns.

The first step to recognizing how to adjust to these changes is recognizing the volatility of markets. Volatility may lead to significant changes in candlestick formations, which can impact their reliability and trading results based on the candlestick. For example, high volatility typically results in longer wicks and larger candle bodies, which can distort traditional patterns and provide false signals. Such a distortion of volatility necessitates a recalibration of pattern recognition strategies to ensure the precision of trade predictions.

In order to man oeuvre in these rough seas, traders have to attain a heightened sense of observation and malleability in their course of action. One of these strategies involves modifying filters and confirmation conditions used in pattern analysis. When volatility is high, traders may use longer timeframes to smooth out the noise, allowing them to see the broader trend. This method helps separate artificial market trends from false fluctuations, which can lead to costly mistakes.

Additionally, the timing of the trades becomes a critical factor in adjusting to market changes. There are periods of the day or week that are more volatile, such as when the market opens or a session overlaps, which can affect the accuracy of candlestick patterns. It is the responsibility of traders to recognize when such periods occur and adjust their strategies accordingly, perhaps by increasing their stop-loss margins or adjusting their position size to manage risk better.

Another vital point in adapting to market changes is the process of incorporating additional tools and indicators to complement candlestick analysis. Moving averages, such as these, can provide a broader picture of the trend and offer additional confirmation of candlestick patterns. Volume analysis is also vital, with the power of a pattern usually confirmed by massive trading volumes and, perhaps, by divergence, which points to the possibility of a turnaround or a fake out.

Essentially, effective trading adaptation is characterized by the readiness to learn and refine strategies on a regular basis. It is not just responding to observed changes, but also predicting them through careful analysis and foresight. Traders should maintain an elaborate journal, keeping records of their trades and the market's environmental factors. The practice helps identify trends in volatility and adjust strategies to ensure they are more aligned with changing market conditions.

Finally, adaptability to market changes extends beyond technical changes to also a mindset that accepts uncertainty and uses it as a growth opportunity. By being informed, flexible, and proactive, traders are better equipped to navigate the complexities of modern markets with greater confidence and strength.

Advanced Study Resources

The trip into the complex world of candlestick analysis can be as thrilling as it is overwhelming. The more one wades into the business of trade, the more one is motivated to have advanced study materials. These materials are not extras; they are the items that provide traders with the level of knowledge needed to master the intricacies of financial markets without hesitation or error.

Books remain an essential element of higher learning, offering a richer understanding that would not normally be found elsewhere. For those who wish to delve deeper into the intricacies of candlestick patterns, a reading list can be invaluable. The list may include the names of books that delve into the historical development of candlestick charts, the psychology behind the formation of patterns, and the incorporation of candlestick analysis with other technical analysis tools. These books often provide case studies and practical examples that shed more light on how theoretical concepts can be applied in real-world situations.

Another option for advanced learning is Webinars and online courses. These sites offer the benefit of live interaction with experienced professionals, who can provide immediate responses and explanations of challenging theories. The range of topics discussed during the webinars is quite wide, starting with the simplest aspects of pattern recognition and progressing to more complex patterns of how candlestick analysis can be combined with alternative trading strategies. Attending these sessions may enhance knowledge of market dynamics and introduce new insights into the interpretation of patterns.

Podcasts have emerged as a valuable source of information for traders on the go. Such audio materials typically include interviews with successful traders and market analysts who share their views and strategies. These conversations can be listened to acquire subtle information on market trends and the psychology of trading, both of which are indispensable towards learning how to master candlestick patterns.

Interacting with highly qualified teachers and guides can significantly accelerate the learning process. These individuals offer customized advice and may help fine-tune your approach to candlestick analysis. Mentors can guide traders in avoiding common pitfalls and establishing a disciplined trading routine by providing personalized feedback and sharing their own experiences.

In addition to personal learning, community involvement is crucial to the learning process. Social media communities and forums dedicated to trading provide a platform for exchanging ideas, discussing strategies, and receiving feedback. It can be beneficial to join such communities to receive support and motivation, making the learning process more interactive and less lonely.

Besides, keeping a trading journal is a priceless practice of constant improvement. The measurement of trades and their review helps determine the patterns of success and identify areas that require improvement. This will help you develop a better appreciation of trading patterns and psychological reactions to market trends, which is imperative for formulating a solid trading plan.

Lastly, but no less importantly, is the aspect of balance in the pursuit of mastery. Constant learning must be supported by the habit of avoiding burnout, which can be achieved by taking frequent breaks, exercising regularly, and practicing meditation. Such routines help keep the mind alert and calm; this is essential for making effective decisions in the fast-paced trading world.

Summing up, numerous complex study resources supplement the path to mastering candlestick analysis. Through books, webinars, podcasts, mentorship, community participation, and personal reflection, traders can develop a deep understanding of market dynamics and enhance their confidence and accuracy in trading.

13

PSYCHOLOGY AND DISCIPLINE IN TRADING

Understanding Emotional Pitfalls

The world of trading is commonly viewed as a battlefield, not necessarily a battle of figures and graphs, but a battle of emotions and psychology. The complex drawings of candlestick patterns and their historical significance are not only a simple indicator of market direction, but also a reflection of the emotional undertones of the traders themselves. Each candlestick pattern narrates a tale of fear, greed, hope, and despair, which sums up the prevailing sentiment of everyone in the market at a particular time.

The most important point is the emotional terrain of the trader, a sophisticated network of psychological traps that can ruin even the most thought-out schemes. Novice traders are often at the mercy of such emotions, driven by the intoxication of easy profits or fear of impending losses. Here is where the real challenge to trading lies —a challenge that is not so much about technical dexterity, but rather about coming to terms with the inner self.

Overconfidence is one of the pitfalls of emotions that is the most frequent and, at the same time, a very dangerous attitude that can lead traders to take unnecessary risks. This usually arises because of a series of successful deals, where the trader starts to think that they are infallible. However, the market is a dynamic creature, and what success you achieve today might not be the same tomorrow. The problem is that overconfidence may cause traders to become blind to this fact, leading them to ignore market changes and warning signals.

Fear, on the other hand, is equally paralyzing. A fear of loss may lead to reluctance to take advantage of good deals, causing traders to miss opportunities to capitalize on them. It may also take the form of panic selling when traders rush out of the market during a negative turn, and in such situations, losses may be crystallized that could have been recouped. The unpredictable nature of markets, which can cause sudden price changes due to market volatility, often intensifies this fear-based behavior, as flight-or-fight instincts can be triggered.

Besides overconfidence and fear, traders are usually faced with the temptation of revenge trading. This happens when a trader, who has suffered a loss, tries to recoup their money as quickly as possible by making even riskier bets. It is an emotional response that can be a slippery slope, and the result is an increasing number of losses as the trader tries to recover what was lost more desperately. The market, which is indifferent to the trader's condition, continues on its own rhythm, often penalizing anyone who tries to adapt to its emotional demands.

It is crucial to be aware of these emotional traps in order to become a successful trader in the long run. It involves a dedication to emotional regulation, recognizing psychological biases, and developing methods to manage them. This can involve establishing strict trading rules, adopting stop-loss orders to control risk, and keeping a journal to reflect on both successful and unsuccessful trades.

Finally, it is a mastery of oneself, just as it is a mastery of the market, when it comes to the journey of learning to use candlestick patterns. By being aware of these emotional traps and addressing them, traders can develop a resilient, disciplined, and adaptive mindset. It is this psychological strength, combined with technical prowess, that makes the difference between a successful trading career and one that navigates a stormy market.

Strengthening Trading Discipline

Discipline is not a nice aspect in trading, but a fundamental pillar of success. The disciplined trader follows a systematic process with rules and strategies that minimize emotional decision-making and enhance consistency. The primary aspect of enhancing trading discipline is the ability to comprehend and effectively manage risk, and to execute every trade according to a clear plan and risk tolerance.

Risk per trade is one of the basic principles of trading discipline. This is achieved by determining the amount of capital at risk based on the size of the overall account and the specific candlestick formation being considered. Following the 1-2% risk rule on each trade allows the trader to avoid losing their account on a single trade. This is a very conservative approach that is crucial for retaining capital in the long term and avoiding devastating losses.

Another important element is adjusting risk according to the pattern of confidence. Before a trader commits capital, they need to consider the quality and reliability of a candlestick pattern. There can be high-confidence setups that merit a fraction of increased risk within the established parameters, while lower-confidence setups may attract more cautious operating or be avoided altogether.

In disciplined trading, position sizing is a very crucial ability that is determined by the stop-loss distance and the preset amount of risk. Traders can determine the position size by using a formula, such as dividing the account risk by the risk per share or the risk per pip. This ensures that every trade is conducted in accordance with the general risk management plan and that there is no excessive exposure to market volatility.

Another practice of a disciplined approach to trading is setting clear risk-reward ratios. This involves trading in areas where the reward is likely to be greater than the risk, and often follows a 2:1 minimum rule. This ensures that successful trades have the capacity to offset potential losses, thereby boosting overall profitability.

The placement of a stop-loss is a crucial part of trading discipline. Higher techniques include laying stops above invalidation points of a pattern, such as below the wick of a hammer or above the high of a shooting star. This strategy will prevent early exits because of market noise and increase the consistency of the stop-loss order. Adapting stop-loss strategies to market conditions and asset volatility is also necessary, and instruments such as the Average True Range (ATR) are used to make them dynamic.

Disciplined trading is another aspect of managing the losing trades. Professionals do not perceive losses as failures, but rather as opportunities for learning and refinement. It is this attitude that enables traders to learn from their mistakes, whether it be a flawed pattern, market situation, or execution, and make the necessary changes. Another essential part of the solution is to incorporate a post-trade analysis process that can help detect and address recurring problems, transforming losses into growth opportunities.

Lastly, the disciplined trader maintains a trading journal to monitor their performance, emotions, and adherence to the trading plan. The practice promotes continuous improvement and accountability, enabling traders to recognize their strengths and weaknesses, as well as areas that need strategic improvement. By adhering to a strict strategy, traders will feel more confident and resilient through the market's intricacies and ultimately, become more consistent and successful in their trading activities.

Stress Management Techniques

Stress is an unwelcome companion in the world of trading, which is fast and hectic. Anxiety can be caused by the need to make quick decisions, market uncertainty, and the risk of financial loss, which traders may experience. To cope with such a challenging environment, it is crucial to implement effective stress management measures.

Among the easiest yet most effective methods is creating a routine with regular breaks. Taking breaks now and then, as traders step away from their screens, can help prevent burnout and maintain mental clarity. This will not only help curb stress but also enable traders to re-enter the market with a renewed attitude, allowing them to make more informed decisions.

In addition to taking breaks, practicing mindfulness and breathing exercises can significantly help reduce stress levels. Mindfulness, including meditation, helps traders focus on the present moment and minimize the emotional impact of market volatility on them. Even the simplest kind of breathing exercises, conducted before and during trading sessions, can be beneficial in relaxing the mind and ensuring it remains focused, which acts as a buffer against the emotional ups and downs of trading.

Journaling is another effective technique that serves as a tool for reflection and emotional control. Traders can identify patterns that cause stress and address them proactively by recording their trades, emotions, and thought processes. Journaling is also a source of historical record that traders can study to understand how to improve on previous experiences, solidify positive habits, and reduce negative ones.

Another key pillar of effective stress management is regular physical activity. Regular physical exercise not only improves physical health but also enhances the mental state, as it releases endorphins, which are natural stress-relievers in the body. It can be a brisk walk, a gym session, or a yoga session, but incorporating physical activity into the daily routine can play a significant role in alleviating stress and enhancing overall performance levels.

Additionally, stress can be alleviated by setting achievable objectives and maintaining a realistic outlook on trading outcomes. Traders can be helped to stay emotionally balanced by understanding that losses are a normal part of the trading process and that the primary aim is to grow and rise over time, rather than to fall short in the short term. This change of perspective helps traders become more resilient, allowing them to enter every session with a calm and focused attitude.

Community support is also an important component in stress management. This can be achieved by networking with other traders in forums or local groups, which brings a sense of camaraderie and shared experience. Talking about the difficulties and sharing stress management coping strategies can provide new information and help build a supportive support system, which helps to eliminate the feeling of isolation, which may increase stress.

Lastly, it is essential to get sufficient rest and maintain a healthy work-life balance. Sleep loss can affect judgment and stress levels; therefore, rest is essential for traders. By setting limits on trading and personal life, traders can keep their mental health at the forefront and prevent stress from overwhelming their everyday lives.

To conclude, effective stress management in trading involves developing a comprehensive strategy that encompasses all aspects, including mental, physical, and emotional. By incorporating these methods into their everyday work, traders will be able to be more resilient and perform better, ensuring that stress does not become a barrier to success that overpowers them.

Building Emotional Resilience

In the dynamic and ever-changing environment of trading, where swift and sometimes urgent decisions are required, one's emotional resilience can be the key to success or failure. Emotional resilience in trading is not just about controlling yourself in highly stressful situations, but also about cultivating a mindset that is both flexible and resilient in response to market fluctuations.

The fundamental principle of developing emotional resilience is that trading is inherently unpredictable. By recognizing this uncertainty, traders can expect anything at each session, thereby making unexpected changes in market movements less emotional. This is not a preparation to help you get rid of your emotions, but to cope with them. Through cultivating a heightened sense of responsiveness to market stressors, traders can train themselves to react calmly to market stimuli with calculated results, rather than spontaneous responses.

Mindfulness is one of the effective strategies that have been developed to increase emotional resilience. This entails being present in the moment and not judging oneself. To traders, mindfulness can be a powerful tool to avoid letting fear and greed drive their trading decisions. Different methods, such as deep breathing, meditation, or taking a quick pause before executing a trade, can provide the necessary space to re-examine a situation objectively.

Besides mindfulness, a regular schedule can also significantly enhance emotional strength. A regular break, healthy food intake, and a physical activity routine can contribute to a balanced lifestyle, which, in turn, facilitates mental clarity and emotional stability. For traders, this can include planned off-screen rest times, time to reflect, and recover.

The other essential element of emotional resilience is that we should be able to learn from our lessons, regardless of whether they are successes or failures, without being emotionally invested in the outcome. This includes treating every trade as a lesson, where one concentrates on the process rather than the outcome. In this aspect, journaling may be especially useful, as it enables traders to monitor their emotional reactions and adjust their approaches over time, drawing on previous experience.

The other crucial factor in developing emotional resilience is peer support. By joining a group of traders, one will be in a position to share experiences, gain new knowledge about trading, and receive support when going through tough times. The feeling of belonging and support can be extremely reassuring, regardless of whether it is in online forums, trading groups, or mentoring relationships.

Ultimately, developing emotional strength in trading involves cultivating a personal approach that combines emotional control with trading expertise. This individual plan must be flexible and may change and evolve as one gains experience in the markets. Traders can better withstand the vagaries of the market by emphasizing emotional resilience as a central feature of their trading strategy, and in doing so, they are more likely to navigate market complexities with confidence and skill.

14

CONCLUSION AND NEXT STEPS

Recap of Key Concepts

The complex nature of candlestick charting requires that any trader wishing to have clarity and accuracy of their trading strategies must know the basic terms used in the process. The candlestick charts and their visual narration provide a glimpse into the psychology of the market and the ongoing war between buyers and sellers. A candlestick is a concise representation of market sentiment, showing the open, close, high, and low prices over a specified time period. The candlestick body represents the trading range between the open and the close, whereas the wicks, or shadows, represent the limit of the trading activity in that time.

A bullish candlestick, typically characterized by a white or green body, indicates that the closing price was higher than the opening price, suggesting a buying force or bullish sentiment. A bearish candlestick, typically depicted in black or red, on the other hand, indicates that the closing price was lower than the opening price, indicating selling pressure or bearishness. Additional information can be gained through the length of the body and the length of the wicks. A long body is a strong indication of buying or selling power, while long wicks could indicate market indecision or a possible reversal.

The major trends in candlestick charting, such as bullish engulfing, hammer, and shooting star, are indicators of possible reversals or continuations in the market. An example of a bullish engulfing pattern is illustrated, where the large body is white, and the smaller body is black, indicating a potential reversal from a downtrend to an uptrend. The hammer, with a small body and a long lower wick, suggests a possible bullish reversal, particularly when it appears at the end of a downward trend. Instead, the shooting star, having its small body and long upper wick, is a possible bearish reversal when it occurs at the summit of an uptrend.

The recognition of these patterns requires more than just a glance at the shapes on the chart; it involves interpreting the market sentiment that the pattern represents. This is an important interpretation for informed trading. An example is that a price move in a high-volume environment may have a greater impact compared to a low-volume market, as volume can validate a price move.

Additionally, the setting in which a pattern occurs is important. The patterns are to be studied in relation to the general market direction and in conjunction with other technical indicators to ensure their authenticity. This strategy will enable traders to avoid false signals and enhance the reliability of their trading strategies.

It is essential to reiterate these key points, which emphasize the role of candlestick charting as a valuable tool for traders. It provides a pictorial and intuitive way to understand market sentiment and make informed decisions. Through a mastery of the fundamentals of candlestick anatomy and an understanding of the psychology of candlesticks, traders are better equipped to navigate the complexities of the financial markets by viewing candlestick patterns not as isolated signals, but as components of an overall trading strategy. The knowledge gained here serves as a stepping stone towards more advanced candlestick analysis and success in trading.

Applying Knowledge in Live Markets

To survive in the complex world of live markets, one must apply theoretical knowledge into practice. This shift is not simply one of identifying patterns in candlesticks under ideal conditions, but rather one of appreciating the changing patterns in real-time trading situations. In live markets, each candlestick represents a complex interplay of market psychology, where traders must derive meaning not only from the pattern itself but also from the broader market context.

One important thing that can be done to ensure knowledge is applied is to develop a keen sense of time. This entails the ability to judge when to enter and exit trades, which is usually determined by the pace of opening and closing hours in the market. For example, the first hour of the U.S. stock market, also commonly referred to as the power hour, is characterized by a higher level of volatility, which can bring both opportunities and risks. The midday lull, on the other hand, can result in less activity and possibly false signals. This knowledge of these time dynamics helps traders match their strategies with the high-reliability periods.

Furthermore, traders should adjust their strategy according to the specific asset class they are trading. Each of the stocks, forex, and cryptocurrencies is associated with its own set of difficulties and behavioral peculiarities. For example, foreign exchange markets can undergo unexpected shifts on days of economic announcements, whereas cryptocurrencies are notorious for their volatility over weekends due to lower liquidity. This process involves adapting to such circumstances, which entails adjusting stop-losses, recalibrating position size, and occasionally modifying the pattern itself that one wishes to trade.

In live markets, risk management is the most important thing. One should not only identify a pattern but also determine the right amount of risk to take. This entails computing the sizes of positions based on the asset's volatility and the trader's risk tolerance. It is a common practice to bet a fixed percentage of the trading account on every trade, ensuring that no single loss can significantly impact the overall portfolio.

Market psychology is another essential skill for interpreting candlestick patterns in live markets. Every candle is a tale of the eternal struggle between buyers and sellers, and how the sentiment changes and where it may turn. To illustrate, a long bottom wick could be taken as a strong defense by buyers, and a succession of small-bodied candles may be a sign of indecision.

Traders should also learn to sift through the noise, including irrelevant price movements that can distort the market's direction. This should be done by concentrating on patterns that have been proven reliable and adjusting the strategies to suit market conditions. Multi-timeframe analysis may be especially useful, as it enables traders to validate higher-timeframe patterns, thereby eliminating low-quality signals on lower timeframes.

Ultimately, the application of knowledge in live markets and its successful implementation depend on the trader's flexibility and adaptability. Markets are constantly evolving, and what works in one situation may not work in another. It requires continuous learning and adaptation based on real-time feedback and post-trade analysis. A disciplined approach to thinking, combined with technical and psychological understanding, can help traders successfully navigate the realities of live markets and transform theory into practical outcomes.

Setting Personal Trading Goals

Goal-setting in trading is one of the pillars of the trading world that shapes the path of any trader. It begins with reflecting on oneself and one's wishes and concludes with the creation of a very specific plan to follow. The purpose of establishing personal trading objectives is to gain clarity about what you actually desire to accomplish in your trading activities and then develop a roadmap to achieve those goals.

One of the most important aspects of having these goals is having a vision that extends beyond financial gain. Although profit is the primary objective, personal development and skill improvement should also be given prominence. This is a holistic approach that motivates traders even during difficult periods. It entails questioning why trading matters, what successful trading would look like, and how it fits into the overall goals of life.

Defining personal trading goals can be broken down into several steps. First of all, it involves immersing oneself in the world of self-awareness. This includes recognizing one's strengths and weaknesses, understanding one's risk tolerance, and identifying the types of trading that best align with one's lifestyle and personality. Through such considerations, traders will be able to establish realistic and attainable goals tailored to their individual situations.

Once self-awareness has been achieved, the next step is to define specific, measurable, attainable, relevant, and time-bound (SMART) goals. These objectives serve as a map, providing direction and guidance. An example is that a trader may have a target to gain a specific percentage of the investment within a given time period, or to have mastered a particular trading strategy by the end of the year. These objectives should be written down and periodically reviewed to monitor progress and make any necessary adjustments.

Along with formulating long-term objectives, it is also necessary to establish short-term goals that serve as milestones towards achieving bigger objectives. These may be in the form of daily or weekly goals, such as a specific number of hours to spend on market research or a certain number of practice trades. Short-term goals provide direct attention and allow for the continuation of momentum by offering frequent opportunities for success and reflection.

Another important element in formulating personal trading objectives is to commit to a culture of continuous improvement. The trading environment is volatile, and traders should be flexible enough to adapt and evolve. This will entail staying up-to-date with market trends, experiencing both successes and failures, and seeking learning materials to enhance trading skills. Traders can cultivate a culture of learning and adaptation to refine their strategies and enhance performance.

Furthermore, personal trading objectives are also expected to incorporate risk management elements. This entails establishing acceptable loss parameters, setting stop-loss orders, and determining an acceptable position size that fits within a person's risk tolerance. Effective risk management has the benefit of making traders resilient to market changes without affecting their overall strategy.

Lastly, creating personal trading objectives is also never an individual undertaking. Trading communities, which seek mentorship and share experiences with other traders, can be valuable and helpful. Such interactions can be used to refine objectives, provide accountability and motivation through shared experiences, and support.

To summarize, setting personal trading goals is a complex process that requires introspection, planning, and reflection. Traders can find purpose and confidence in navigating the complex world of trading by setting goals tailored to their personal values and market realities. The strategic approach not only increases the likelihood of financial success but also helps the person develop and ultimately fulfill the trading journey.

Invitation to the Trading Community

The trading world, similar to a busy shopping center, can be overwhelmed by a plethora of voices, each vying to be heard with offers of tricks and tips. The trader, to find his way out of this din, may be a mariner groping his way through a sea of never-ending waves. However, within this pool of information lies the lighthouse of candlestick patterns — a time-tested instrument that provides order and orientation.

With their illustrious past in Japanese rice trading, candlestick charts offer a visual representation of the market's psychology and the spirit of buyer-seller interactions. One story in each candlestick represents a mini-historical world that reflects the general mood of all its members at a specific time. To traders, understanding this language is akin to grasping the language of the marketplace, a necessary skill for deciphering the nuances of market trends.

The entry into the trading community, informed by candlestick analysis, suggests that one welcomes a tradition of uniting technical accuracy with intuition. In this case, the trader does not sit back and watch the markets; rather, he is an active participant in the drama unfolding in the markets. The candlestick chart becomes a canvas, and trends such as the bullish engulfing or the doji are brushstrokes that create a picture of possible trends and reversals.

This is not a call to be a spectator, but to be an active participant. It prompts traders to delve into the intricacies of pattern recognition, with every candlestick contributing to a larger, more complex puzzle. It is not merely a matter of recognizing shapes by name, but rather requires an appreciation of context, volume, and market conditions. It is the power of seeing the pattern behind the story, anticipating its consequences, and making informed choices on a combination of historical information and real-time analysis.

Furthermore, the trading community thrives on the mutual knowledge and experience of its members. Interacting with other traders, whether in forums, webinars, or study groups, is a way to enhance one's knowledge and gain different perspectives on pattern interpretation and strategy formulation. The wisdom of the crowd is an important aspect of a trader's development, as it provides insights that cannot be detected through individual analysis.

Continuous learning and adaptation is also a call that is in the invitation. Markets are dynamic, constantly changing, and what is true today might not be true tomorrow. In this way, traders are motivated to be lifelong students of the market, constantly upgrading their techniques and strategies. This does not just mean learning new patterns and techniques, but also considering previous trades to learn from both successes and failures.

This invitation to the trading community, in essence, is an invitation to lifelong learning and mastery. It is not avoiding the difficulties and benefits of trading, but rather having them guided by the clarity of candlestick patterns. By accepting this invitation, traders will embark on a course of self-discipline, critical thinking, and social interactions, all geared towards achieving a higher degree of clarity and success in the trading field.

EPILOGUE

As we draw the final curtain on "Candlestick Clarity," it's essential to reflect on the transformative power these pages hold for those willing to delve into the world of market psychology and pattern recognition. This book has been more than just a guide; it has been a catalyst for change, a companion on the road to mastering the art of reading market sentiment through the language of candlesticks.

Throughout this journey, readers have been equipped with the tools to decipher the intricate dance between bulls and bears, uncovering the hidden narratives that each candlestick tells. By focusing on the psychological underpinnings of market movements, we have laid the groundwork for a deeper understanding of trading that extends beyond mere price action. This approach not only demystifies the cluttered charts but also instills confidence in making informed decisions.

The strategies and insights shared here are designed to empower traders to look beyond the surface, recognize the subtle shifts in momentum, and anticipate the traps set by market euphoria or panic. Each pattern, each sequence of candles, becomes a story, a narrative that speaks of past struggles and future possibilities. The ability to read these stories accurately can mean the difference between a successful trade and a missed opportunity.

Furthermore, the emphasis on real-world application, through annotated examples and platform-specific tutorials, ensures that theory seamlessly translates into practice. By fostering a disciplined approach to pattern recognition and trade execution, this book encourages traders to develop their unique style and strategy, tailored to their individual goals and market preferences.

In embracing the lessons of "Candlestick Clarity," traders are not just learning a skill; they are adopting a mindset that prioritizes continuous learning and adaptation. The market is ever-changing, and so must be the trader. The courage to adapt, the commitment to practice, and the resilience to learn from every outcome are the hallmarks of a trader who is not just reactive but proactive.

As readers close this chapter and step back into the bustling world of trading, they do so with a newfound clarity. A clarity that cuts through the noise, that sees opportunity where others see chaos, and that empowers them to trade with precision and confidence. With candlestick clarity, the market is no longer an enigma but a canvas, ready to be read and mastered.